Children's Errors in Mathematics

Second edition

Children's Errors in Mathematics

Understanding common misconceptions in
primary schools

Second edition

Edited by Alice Hansen

LearningMatters

First published in 2005 by Learning Matters Ltd
Reprinted in 2005
Reprinted in 2007
Reprinted in 2008 (twice)
Reprinted in 2009
Reprinted in 2010
Second edition published in 2011

British Library Cataloguing in Publication Data
A CIP record for this book is available from the British Library.

ISBN: 978 1 84445 612 3

This book is also available in following ebook formats:
Adobe ebook ISBN: 978 1 84445 7 694
EPUB ebook ISBN: 978 1 84445 7 687
Kindle ISBN: 978 0 8725 0 254

Cover and text design by Code 5 Design Associates Ltd
Project Management by Deer Park Productions.
Typeset by Pantek Arts, Maidstone, Kent.
Printed and bound in Great Britain by Bell & Bain Ltd, Glasgow

Learning Matters Ltd
20 Cathedral Yard
Exeter EX1 1HB
Tel: 01392 215560
info@learningmatters.co.uk
www.learningmatters.co.uk

Mixed Sources
Product group from well-managed
forests and other controlled sources
www.fsc.org Cert no. TT-COC-002769
© 1996 Forest Stewardship Council
FSC

Contents

About the editor and contributors

Editor

Alice Hansen

Alice Hansen is an educational consultant who has taught in a wide variety of primary schools in England and abroad. She worked for over a decade in Initial Teacher Education (ITE) as a senior lecturer in primary mathematics education at the University of Cumbria (formerly St Martin's College) before becoming the Programme Leader for the full time primary Postgraduate Certificate in Education with Qualified Teacher Status. Since becoming a consultant, she has worked with a significant number of ITE providers across England, supporting the development of their mathematics education courses. Alice is also the director of Children Count Ltd, through which she remains active in researching children's mathematics learning and wider educational issues to support ITE provision nationally.

Contributors

Doreen Drews

Doreen Drews taught extensively within the Foundation Stage, Key Stage 1 and Key Stage 2. She was a mathematics advisory teacher for four years before joining St Martin's College (now University of Cumbria). She has a particular interest in Early Years mathematics, and how resources can be used to support children's mathematical understanding effectively.

John Dudgeon

John Dudgeon is the primary mathematics subject leader at the University of Cumbria. He has taught at a wide range of primary schools. John is particularly interested in mathematical development in children in the Early Years Foundation Stage and in the effective use of mathematical resources.

Fiona Lawton

Fiona Lawton has taught in a range of primary and secondary schools. She is the University of Cumbria programme leader for the Graduate Teacher Programme. Her main interests include developing online materials to support teaching and learning in mathematics and she is researching the underpinning pedagogy of e-learning.

Liz Surtees

Liz Surtees is the Assessment Officer at Bute Medical School, University of St Andrews. She has taught mathematics across the primary and secondary school age ranges, in further education and higher education contexts. She is particularly interested in statistics and problem solving and is co-author of *Mathematics Across the Curriculum – Problem solving, reasoning and numeracy in primary schools* and Fox, S and Surtees, L (2010) Breaking down the boundaries. *Teach Primary!* Vol. 4.6, pp88–91.

Introduction

This book has been written as a resource for you to develop your knowledge and understanding about children's mathematical conceptual development and how errors and misconceptions are a natural part of learning mathematics.

Using this book

You can use this book in a number of ways, which are outlined below.

1 **Planning:** When you are planning a lesson or unit of work, Chapters 3 onwards can be used as a reference guide to help you to consider some of the possible misconceptions and errors the children you are working with may exhibit. If your planning takes into consideration some of the possible misconceptions the children may show, you will be better prepared in your teaching.
2 **Teaching**: As well as feeling more confident in your teaching because of your thorough planning, at times you may present some of the examples in this book with the children you are teaching. This can offer an opportunity for rich mathematical discussion about a potentially difficult aspect in a context that is 'safe' for the children. Additionally, Chapters 1 and 2 may challenge your perception of what errors and misconceptions are, and ultimately this may help you to shape how you teach children.
3 **Children's assessment**: By being able to identify misconceptions and discuss these with children, you will be able to use these opportunities as they present themselves as an excellent Assessment for Learning opportunity.
4 **Your own coursework**: This book will support coursework you are required to complete for your teaching qualification. In addition to assignments directly related to errors and misconceptions, you will also find other supporting material such as theories on how children learn mathematics and ways of teaching mathematics effectively.
5 **Subject knowledge**: Although this book addresses many of the common errors and misconceptions that you may see in primary schools, you may find that you also develop your own subject knowledge by thinking through them as you plan, teach and assess.

Chapter 1 sets the scene for the remainder of the book. It is important for you to understand why and how misconceptions arise because through understanding, your planning, teaching and assessment will improve. In Chapter 2, Doreen Drews develops these ideas and discusses the role of the student teacher who is following this misconceptions-aware teaching approach. The remaining chapters present a number of common errors that children will exhibit during their Early Years Foundation Stage and primary years. In order to make the most of this book, it is essential that you note the following.

1 These errors can be demonstrated by any child, regardless of their attainment level and their age.
2 These errors, while presented in one context in this book, can be often seen in a multitude of mathematical contexts. Cross-references are included as appropriate.

3 Mathematical errors can be observed within mathematics lessons, or just as frequently in sessions or lessons that have a less mathematical focus. For example, a science lesson that explores plant growth or a DT lesson requiring accuracy of measurement both require children to be able to use a ruler accurately and record using the appropriate units of measurement.

4 The discussion of each misconception involves some common reasons why the error may have been made. However, the discussion may not be exhaustive and you should look for alternatives during your own work with children.

The Appendix offers busy students on placement experiences the opportunity to dip in and out of the errors as they plan in relation to the curriculum or framework objectives.

How do children learn mathematics?

Alice Hansen

Chapter overview

Understanding how children learn mathematics is a critical element of your beginning to understand the errors and misconceptions they make. This chapter aims to support you to:

- develop your understanding of children's mathematical cognitive development (the micro-level);
- develop your understanding of cognitive development within mathematics curricula (the macro-level);
- understand that all children (and adults, too) make errors in their mathematics work as they construct their own mis-conceptions of mathematics;
- identify that adults mediate learning for children.

Distinguishing between macro-level and micro-level cognitive development

As a teacher you will be working within two levels of cognitive development as you plan, teach and assess. At the macro level, you will be ensuring that you meet the statutory requirements of the mathematics curriculum. At the micro level, you will be proactively responding to each individual's needs and considering effective personalised learning for every child in your class. This is challenging to do, even when you become an experienced teacher. It is challenging because the spiral curriculum we use presents mathematical concepts hierarchically. This is evident in the level descriptions that can be found for mathematics (DfEE, 1999a). Through these, the curriculum presents conceptual development as a smooth progression throughout a child's primary years. We can expect most children through their primary years to make steady progress from level 1 to level 4 (or above). However, you will probably know from your own learning experiences and your teaching experience that learning is very much context-dependent, and this has an impact on individual children's progress.

Let's pause to pursue this. A child working at level 3 is able to state the properties of shapes. Do that now for a square.

I suspect you have stated that is has four interior angles of equal size (all 90°) and four sides of equal length. It is likely that you thought about the order of rotation and number of lines of symmetry (and linked these to the square being a regular polygon with four sides). You may have also visualised the square having equal-length diagonals that are perpendicular. These numerous properties satisfy at least part of the level 3 National Curriculum level description (DfEE, 1999a).

Now do this with a less familiar shape, such as a kite. You may wish to use these prompts to help you. Using an **inclusive definition** of a kite, what are the:

- number of right angles?
- number of pairs of equal and opposite angles?
- number of pairs of equal and opposite sides?
- number of equal-length sides?
- number of pairs of parallel sides?
- number of lines of symmetry?
- number of perpendicular diagonals?
- number of equal-length diagonals?
- number of bisecting diagonals?
- what is the order of rotation?

How did you get on? Check your answers with those on page 10. I suspect when you were carrying out the task, you had a prototypical picture of a kite in your mind (see Figure 1.1). That might be why you (probably) stated that the kite had just one line of symmetry. However, if we are considering the properties of a kite using inclusive definitions, remember a square is also a type of kite (see Figure 1.2). Therefore, if you were using an inclusive definition of 'kite', you should have stated that a kite has 'at least one line of symmetry', or that it has 'an order of rotation of at least 1'.

Am I confusing you? I hope so. (The notion of inclusivity is something that children – and adults – find difficult. See, for example, Jones (2000), Hansen and Pratt (2005), Hansen (2008).) My point is that when we track children's progress over time, it appears smooth and (often) reflects the expectations of the prescribed curriculum. However, when we take a close look at a moment in that learning journey in detail, we no longer see a smooth development. Instead we observe oscillation which is all rather messy. This is represented in Figure 1.3.

Figure 1.1: A prototypical kite

Figure 1.2: More examples of kites

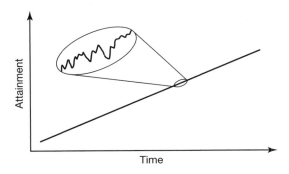

Figure 1.3: Macro- and micro-level cognitive change

One final example, described by Simpson (2009, page 15), may help to describe this phenomenon:

> Shaun had successfully measured a number of pencils and had been able to record their lengths in order; he knew that 21.4cm was longer than 21.25cm. However, in another lesson later in the same week, he was ordering a list of numbers and stated that 13.65 was bigger than 13.7.

What does this tell you about Shaun's mathematical understanding of number (decimals), measurement (length) and use and application of mathematics? What does it tell you about his attainment at the macro-level and at the micro-level?

Macro- and micro-level cognitive change: planning and assessment

Macro- and micro-level cognitive change is seen reflected in a number of the aspects of a primary teacher's role. Two of these are planning and assessment. Although these two aspects are strongly interrelated, Table 1.1 provides a summary of these discretely in order to exemplify them.

	Macro-level	**Micro-level**
Planning	Follows long-term curriculum learning objectives	Follows short-term unit/weekly/lesson learning objectives
	Provides an overview of a yearly/termly/half-termly **intended** learning journey	Identifies learning outcomes based on **actual** data gathered about very recent outcomes
	Focuses on a larger group of children (typically the whole class, a year group or in some instances a key stage)	Focuses on a smaller group of children or individuals

	Macro-level	Micro-level
Planning	Planning focuses mainly on content and context/themes	Planning considers how the content is learned, e.g. learning styles, resources, grouping, etc.
	Changes may or may not be made to planning	Change is inevitable
	Any changes will be minimal	Changes may be significant
	Any changes will impact on the longer term	Changes will occur **in** lessons and **between** lessons
Assessment	Summative in nature	Formative and diagnostic in nature
	Happens at key points in the year/key stage	Happens continuously
	Assesses children's attainment over a longer term using curriculum levels or part thereof (e.g. 1c, 1b, 1a)	Assesses children's attainment according to short-term learning objectives
	Often uses a limited range of assessment strategies (typically pencil-and-paper tests or 'tasks' carried out independently)	Often uses a wide variety of Assessment for Learning strategies
	Assesses the yearly/termly/half-termly **intended** learning outcomes	Identifies 'next steps' learning outcomes based on recent assessment data gathered
	These are used systematically to inform further long-term planning and to support transition between years	Used spontaneously or systematically to inform pedagogical decisions within a lesson or for the next lesson(s)
	Often used to inform communication to parents at the end of a year	Can be used to inform communication with children, teaching assistants, parents or other adults supporting the child's learning
	Used to inform tracking of individual pupils' progress	Focus on the number of children changes depending on the learning/teaching undertaken
	Can be used to prompt lesson study in a particular area of a teacher's performance	Can be used in lesson study to support professional development through peer support

	Macro-level	Micro-level
Assessment	Assessment focuses on a narrow curriculum	Assessment focuses on a wider range of knowledge, skills or understanding
	Any assessments will impact on the longer term	Any assessments will occur in lessons and **between** lessons

Table 1.1: Comparison of macro- and micro- level planning and assessment

The outcomes associated with macro- and micro-level cognitive change can be seen in many aspects of our teaching. Exploring the literature around these levels helps us to continue to develop our understanding. Therefore, the next section will consider in more detail the two levels. First, it will look at macro-level cognitive change, identifying how the literature represents the hierarchical nature of mathematical learning. Next, the notion of micro-level conceptual change is discussed. This goes on to explore some of the literature related to micro-level conceptual change and offers an explanation for why children make errors and develop 'misconceptions' in mathematics.

Macro-level cognitive change: exploring the notion of hierarchy

The long- and medium-term planning teachers undertake is led by statutory and other curricula which are in part informed by macro-level theories of learning (e.g. Dubinsky *et al.*, 2005; Tall, 2007; Weber, 2005). These are usually hierarchical in nature, involving earlier concepts becoming the foundations for later concepts to be built upon. This can be explained as a process where a new concept becomes developed sufficiently for it to become an object that can be used in a more advanced concept. For example, addition may be seen as an object that can be used in multiplication. Once we know how to calculate $3 + 3 + 3 + 3$, this knowledge can be used to calculate 3×4.

To explain this, we can use the image of a spiral – as Jerome Bruner did – to model how concepts are expanded upon as they are developed. As you read the literature review below, consider what model you have developed in your mind to explain this process and the different terms that are used to explain this.

Many mathematics educators and theorists have written about these ideas. For example, Anna Sfard explored mathematical development taking guidance from mathematics history. She explained that the history of mathematics can be characterised as an *ongoing process of reification in which the processes are reinterpreted as objects* (Sfard, 1991). We can see this through the historical development of mathematics. For example, the evolution of a base-ten number system enabled written calculations to be developed. This is seen in curriculum guidance, where children are expected to have a good understanding of place value and mental calculation before they are taught formal written calculation methods (see, for further guidance, 'Teaching Written Calculations' from QCA, 1999).

Hans Freudenthal is a well-known figure in mathematics education. He was the founder of the Freudenthal Institute in Holland, where the Realistic Mathematics Education (RME) curriculum is being developed. Some aspects of this curriculum, such as the empty number line, have been borrowed within English mathematics non-statutory frameworks and guidance. Freudenthal (1973) proposed that children should develop their mathematical understanding through reinventing mathematics. He suggested that children be given the opportunity to experience a similar process to the way a particular topic of mathematics was invented. He was clear that children should not repeat history as it occurred (Freudenthal, 1981), but rather as if our ancestors had known what we now know. He maintained that conceptual development is psychological, rather than historical, in its progression. Gravemeijer and Doorman (1999), also from the Freudenthal Institute, explain that the core activity within reinvention is 'mathematising', a way of *organising from a mathematical perspective*. Reification is identifiable here because *the operational matter on one level becomes a subject matter on the next level.*

Dubinsky's A-P-O-S theory (Dubinsky *et al.*, 2005) identifies a common cyclic development called encapsulation. This cycle involves four levels whereby the last relates to a combined object-schema that in turn becomes the first level of a new cycle (**A**ctions that are perceived as external, are interiorised into internal **P**rocesses, encapsulated as mental **O**bjects developing within a coherent mathematical **S**chema) (adapted from Poynter and Tall, 2004). Gray and Tall (2007, page 25) explain how the process of compression involves *taking complicated phenomena, focusing on essential aspects of interest to conceive of them as whole to make them available as an entity to think about.*

While this all seems fairly straightforward at the macro-level, what is unclear in all these approaches is the specific point at which a child has reified, reinvented, encapsulated or compressed a concept. For example, you will read in Chapter 3 that Gelman and Gallistel revealed how complex it is for young children to learn to count. Can we say that a child is able to count because they can recite the number labels to ten in order? Or when they can count to 100, or in tens or hundreds, or when they know that counting is an infinite activity? Is it when they can 'count on' in order to add … using integers … fractional numbers…?

At the macro-level, it is possible to identify a qualitative difference between the attainment of children who are five years of age and ten years of age. However, if we focus on an individual child, their attainment is less straightforward. The clear, smooth progression at the macro level appears to give way to apparent fluctuation at the micro level, demonstrating a 'gap' between macro- and micro-level theories of conceptual change (diSessa and Cobb, 2004).

What is micro-level conceptual change?

In the literature review on macro-level conceptual change above it was possible to see that although different theorists use different terminology, there exists a broadly agreed model about the learning of mathematical concepts. This is also observable within the literature about micro-level conceptual change. For example, there is common reference to children cognitively making systematic associations that they develop from their experiences within the rich world around them. This may be thought of as a web, where connections are made between the particular instances (Tennyson, 1996) of a concept that children experience. As these instances become increasingly associated, prototypes (early concepts) are formed.

Similarly, diSessa and Sherin (1998) refer to a co-ordination class. They define it as *systematically connected ways of getting information from the world* (page 1171). This is developed through a process they refer to as *conceptual bootstrapping*. Both of these views of children's early conceptual change rely on children noticing what is happening around them and (usually subconsciously) making connections with other experiences or understanding of the ideas being developed.

Noss and Hoyles (1996, page 105) put forward a case for learning which involves the construction of a web of connections between resources. Resources may be formal or informal, internal (cognitive) and external (physical or virtual). The web is developed through connections being made between these resources. By drawing on the webbing of a particular setting, children will shape the way that they express their mathematical ideas (Noss and Hoyles, 1996, page 122). Noss and Hoyles call this process/object *situated abstraction*. Learners abstract within rather than away from (the literal meaning of 'abstract') a situation, webbing their own knowledge and understanding by acting within the situation.

Wilensky (1991, page 201) also suggests that children establish connections to bring about cognitive change. He sees that this *process of development moves from the abstract to the concrete*. Wilensky labels the process of concretising as *concretion*: the process of new knowledge *coming into relationship with itself and with prior knowledge, and thus becoming concrete*. Wilensky postulates that adults express difficult (higher-order) concepts as abstract because they have little or no understanding of the concept themselves, therefore it is abstract to them. Likewise, the easy (lower-order) concepts are very concrete for them – they understand these concepts because they are grounded. From this, adults then assume that these easier concepts are concrete and as children develop, they move on to more abstract concepts (or, as he calls them, *objects*). Wilensky maintains that all objects are abstract when an individual's relationship with that object is poor. It is only when we use the object in various and multiple ways – when we develop a relationship – that we are able to begin to make sense of it, or it becomes concrete.

Two core aspects emerge from the cognitive change literature. These are the associations (webbing) that enable concretion, and the children's experiences. Chapter 2 deals with children's experiences by discussing in more detail the role of the teacher. How a child develops relationships between resources during concretion or webbing is a process that happens cognitively. Therefore, we can only observe external products of that process, such as verbalised situated abstractions.

Misconceptions and the classroom context

From the literature review on micro-level cognitive change, it is possible to see how misconceptions are inevitable. As situated abstractions develop, or as concretion occurs, children are going to draw on their own understanding of the world around them and unavoidably misconceive some ideas. For example, have you witnessed a young child point to a horse and say 'cow'? They have noticed: (a) an animal in a field; (b) eating grass; (c) swishing its tail; and (d) coloured white and black. These attributes satisfy, for the child, the definition of a cow. They have misconceived the being as a cow. Later they will be able to distinguish between a cow and horse. How can this development be mediated?

The classroom setting is a complex *learning ecology* (Cobb *et al.*, 2003) that *encompasses the historical, cultural, social, and political contexts of both mathematics and mathematics education* (English, 2007, page 122). In the above example, it is likely that an adult or older sibling will correct the young child to explain that the animal is a horse and not a cow.

Cognitive load theory

While misconceptions do occur naturally, it is important for you to be aware that learning can be a laborious (unconscious or conscious) process. Cognitive load theory explains how schemata become automated and become part of our long-term memory. At first, when new information is presented to us, we process it within our working memory, but our working memory is extremely limited in capacity and duration (Miller, 1956; Peterson and Peterson, 1959). Once schemata have transferred from working memory to long-term memory and the information is used, it is not limited (Ericsson and Kintsch, 1995). Information can then be returned to the working memory later to be used efficiently (Tabbers, 2002). In very recent research, Peters (2010) used eye-tracking technology to observe how mathematicians and non-mathematicians work through mathematical problems. He showed how non-experts require explicit processing while they read and interpret mathematics. They tended to read fully all the questions, and after working out the most relevant information, they would check to see if it was actually relevant. Mathematicians, on the other hand, were able to process information effectively by selecting the relevant information very quickly.

Alloway (2006, page 134) undertook a comprehensive literature review that considered how working memory works in the classroom. She identified how *a child with a poor working memory capacity will struggle and often fail in such activities, disrupting and delaying learning* and notes that children with low working memory scores also have poor computational skills. Therefore, Alloway suggests reducing working memory demands in the classroom. This involves:

- ensuring the children know what they are doing (i.e. they can remember the next step);
- reducing processing demands (e.g. simplifying vocabulary);
- breaking down tasks into simpler steps (displaying *aides-mémoire*; encouraging use of memory aids);
- developing effective strategies for coping with situations where a child experiences a failure in working memory.

(adapted from Alloway, 2006, page 138)

Thinking about the process of learning as one which can be mediated in school by the teacher may be helpful. It is likely that you will have already come across Vygotsky's (1978) zone of proximal development (ZPD). It is defined as *the distance between the actual development level as determined by independent problem-solving and the level of potential to development as determined through problem-solving through adult guidance or in collaboration with more capable peers* (Vygotsky, 1978, page 86). The notion of the ZPD was developed by Wood *et al.* (1979), who considered how teachers and peers could build (scaffold) and withdraw (fade) support as necessary to help a child bridge the ZPD.

Cognitive load theory may explain the difference between a 'novice' and an 'expert' (in this case, a child and teacher). Sweller (1988, page 7) explains that the amount of information and how the information is organised are quite different between working memory and long-term memory. He points out that novices *fall back on weak problem-solving strategies ... which leads to a high cognitive load* because they do not have the schemata to support their work.

Vygotsky played a major role in relation to individual and social processes of cognitive change (John-Steiner and Mahn, 2003). Vygotsky understood the power and versatility of speech: *For not only does speech function as a tool that mediates social action, it also [mediates] the individual mental activities of remembering, thinking and reasoning* (Wells, 1999, page 136).

Misconceptions can become rigid and resistant to revision later on (Furani, 2003). Therefore it is the role of teachers to be aware of potential misconceptions, the possible reasons why they have developed (overgeneralisation is common). Doreen Drews discusses the role of the teacher in Chapter 2.

Summary

This chapter has identified two levels of cognitive change. The first is the framework that teachers are required by law to work within: that of macro-level change that can be observed in curricula. Over a child's school career it is likely that a fairly smooth progression through the attainment levels will be mapped out through summative assessments. However, when we place a microscope at any one moment in that child's progression, the cognitive change is no longer smooth. Instead it is messy, with oscillation. You may have experienced this yourself by feeling confused in the kite-defining activity or other mathematics tasks you have undertaken or even taught. Micro-level cognitive change has been explored by many theorists. This chapter has explored the notion of developing situated abstractions and the process of concretion as ways of thinking about how cognitive change occurs.

The chapter has also highlighted how difficult cognitive development can be, by briefly referring to cognitive load theory. The role of the adult in mediating learning concluded this chapter and paves the way for a more detailed discussion of the role of the adult in relation to children's errors and misconceptions in the next chapter.

Inclusive definitions of a kite

On page 2 you were asked to consider the inclusive definition of a kite. It is possible to identify the following attributes of a kite.

Number of right angles?	At least 0
Number of pairs of equal and opposite angles?	At least 1 pair
Number of pairs of equal and opposite sides?	At least 0
Number of equal length sides?	At least 0
Number of pairs of parallel sides?	At least 0
Number of lines of symmetry?	At least 1
Number of perpendicular diagonals?	At least 2
Number of equal length diagonals?	At least 0
Number of bisecting diagonals?	At least 1
What is the order of rotation?	At least 0

Errors and misconceptions: the teacher's role

Doreen Drews

Chapter overview

This chapter explores recent research into teaching approaches to 'deal' with the common mathematical errors and misconceptions made by primary-aged children. It focuses on whether employing teaching approaches which seek to minimise or avoid children making errors and forming misconceptions is likely to be successful. Alternative teaching approaches are considered, based on discussion, dialogue and challenge to children's existing mathematical constructions. Choices and changes in mathematics teaching practices carry with them implications not only for considerations of teaching approaches but also for how teachers view their role within Early Years Foundation Stage settings and Key Stage 1 and Key Stage 2 classrooms.

Distinguishing between mathematical errors and misconceptions

A teacher's response to dealing with a child's mathematical error demands skill in diagnostic terms: different responses will be appropriate depending upon the nature (and frequency) of the error observed.

An error could be made for many reasons. It could be the result of carelessness, misinterpretation of symbols or text, lack of relevant experience or knowledge related to that mathematical topic/learning objective/concept, a lack of awareness or inability to check the answer given, or the result of a misconception. Ryan and Williams (2007, page 16) considered different levels of knowledge and view mathematical errors to be principally formed within surface levels of knowledge: as such, a child's response to a task is procedural and can be corrected by the teacher providing correct alternatives.

In addition to this, Cockburn (1999) discusses the nature of the mathematical tasks selected by the teacher as having potential for children making errors: she suggests that consideration must be given to the complexity of the task (is it sufficiently challenging or too challenging?), the way the task is presented and the ability of the child to *translate* the task, i.e. does the pupil know what is required in mathematical terms? This latter point is fundamental, for example, to a child's ability to solve word problems (see pages 71–74 for more discussion on word problems).

Sometimes errors can be exacerbated by teachers making assumptions about their children's experiences: this has particular resonance for teachers of young children. Some young children may, or may not, have had experiences of handling money, using or observing the use of a balance to measure an item's mass, or 'reading' time on analogue timepieces.

Incorrect uses of resources can lead to children making errors: a number line can only be an effective tool for assisting 'counting on' and 'counting back' if children are shown, and understand, how to count on/back from the first number without including that number in the count. This issue is discussed further on page 62.

The term 'misconception' is discussed in detail in Chapter 1. It is commonly used when a learner's conception is considered to be in conflict with the accepted meanings and understandings in mathematics (Barmby et al., 2009). A misconception could be the misapplication of a rule, an over- or under-generalisation, or an alternative conception of the situation. For example, *a number with three digits is bigger than a number with two digits* works in some situations (e.g. 328 is bigger than 35) but not necessarily in others where decimals are involved (e.g. 3.28 is not bigger than 3.5).

Misconceptions are far more problematic than errors as they are set within deeper levels of knowledge (Ryan and Williams, 2007, page 16). They demand diagnosis and dialogue to ascertain the misconception, which can be time-consuming. Nevertheless, Barmby et al. (2009, page 4) argue that misconceptions should be regarded as *evolving understandings in mathematics ... essential and productive for the development of more sophisticated conceptions and understanding.*

It is important to note that misconceptions are not limited to children who need additional support: more able children also make incorrect generalisations.

Should we teach to hide or avoid mathematical errors and misconceptions?

There is no doubt that some mathematical errors could be avoided by teacher awareness, skilful choice of task and clarity of explanation. However, Swan (2001) suggests that, despite what they are taught, children seem to make the same mathematical errors, and construct their own alternative meanings for mathematics, all over the world. This challenges notions about teaching to avoid children developing such mistakes and misconceptions.

The Primary National Strategy (PNS) advocated diagnosis and intervention schemes that provide *focused teaching activities which tackle fundamental errors and misconceptions that are preventing progress* (DfES, 2005a, page 6). Wave 3 materials emphasised individualised diagnosis of the errors and misconceptions shown by children with significant difficulties, specific or non-specific, with mathematical learning. As Dowker (2009) points out, the focus here is one of using teacher assessment to *correct* identified errors and misconceptions. In order to use Assessment for Learning (AfL) effectively, emphasis also needs to be placed on children recognising themselves that errors and misconceptions are part of the learning process.

Opinions on whether this is possible or even desirable alter from the differing perspectives of primary children and their teachers. Koshy (2000) reports that when primary children were asked how they felt about making mathematical mistakes, they expressed strong feelings of anger, frustration and disappointment. In contrast, Cockburn (1999) and Koshy (2000) both reflect a growing view in the research evidence that mathematical errors can provide a useful insight for teachers into a child's thinking and understanding, an effective mechanism for assessment for learning and, with sensitive handling, can enable children to learn from mathematical mistakes.

Current thinking and research are recommending a shift in how both teachers and children regard mathematical errors and misconceptions, moving from a 'let's plan to avoid' strategy to one which seeks to give greater status and value to diagnosis, explanation and negotiation of meaning. Lee (2006) argues that such strategies lead to more creative approaches to AfL, help pupils see themselves as successful learners and encourage both teachers and pupils to attempt more challenging work. Rather than simply correcting an error or misconception, it would appear far more productive for teachers to investigate the reason a child provides a given answer. Indeed, Barmby *et al.* (2009, page 5) maintain that *identifying and building on incomplete or incorrect conceptions are important ways of developing coherent mathematical knowledge.*

It is self-evident that that such a shift will necessitate teachers adopting *a constructive attitude to their children's mistakes* (Koshy, 2000, page 173), and children recognising that analysis and discussion of mistakes or misconceptions can be helpful to their mathematical development.

Spooner (2002) suggests that placing children in situations where they feel in control of identifying mathematical errors/misconceptions leads to greater openness on the part of the children to explore and discuss their own misconceptions. Working with specifically designed pre-National Test materials for Key Stage 2, he discusses children exploring answers produced by an 'unknown pupil'. In order to do so they had to engage with the mathematical question set, discuss the errors with peers and explore why the error/misconception may have been made. The children appeared willing to engage in such discussions as it wasn't 'their' work under investigation. The process allowed children to be placed in the role of the teacher, encouraged open dialogue and consolidated their understanding of the concepts which underpinned the given examples.

This approach has an underlying belief that children's mathematical understanding is more likely to be developed if children are given opportunities to:

- explain their thinking;
- compare their thinking with that of peers and teachers.

To be effective in terms of long-term gains these opportunities need to be embedded within a school and classroom 'culture' which accepts and promotes that children can learn effectively from their peers and need encouragement to 'be brave' to express their mathematical ideas. Support for this can be found in a report by Ofsted into the Primary National Strategies and their impact upon the rest of the primary curriculum.

> *The most effective teachers ... cultivate an ethos where children do not mind making mistakes because errors are seen as part of the learning. In these cases, children are prepared to take risks with their answers.*
>
> (Ofsted, 2003, page 18)

A significant feature of such approaches would be a recognition by children that learning often involves having to 'shift' one's thinking.

Swan (2001) encourages a more radical shift in teachers' thinking, suggesting that far from trying to teach to avoid children developing misconceptions, the latter should be viewed as helpful and, possibly, 'necessary' stages in children's mathematical development. This suggests that a focus on how children are taught mathematics, rather than on what mathematics they are taught, is needed.

Changing perspectives in this way involves implications for teaching approaches, the way in which mathematical dialogue is 'controlled' by teachers, the role attached to questioning, and the impact of all these considerations on teachers' planning.

Implications for teaching approaches

Research into effective teaching and teachers of numeracy (Askew et al, 1997) highlighted that one factor involved in effective teaching was the emphasis placed on child/teacher discussion. In a school deemed to be one of the most effective in the teaching of numeracy there was a consistent expectation through Key Stage 1 and Key Stage 2 that children would develop skills in explaining their thinking processes: lessons in this school were characterised by dialogue in which teacher and children had to listen carefully to what was being said by others. Significant to this approach was a teacher belief, described as a *connectionist belief*, which views mathematics teaching and learning as something based on a dialogue between teacher and children and is characterised by extensive use of focused discussions in practice. Such a belief has connections with social constructivist perspectives on social and cultural dimensions to learning in which it is recognised that children can learn effectively from others including their peers. Chapter 1 discusses these ideas further.

One concern here for trainee teachers and experienced teachers alike could be the possibility of peer discussion and/or peer collaboration compounding existing mathematical errors and misconceptions through persuasive dialogue. However Anghileri (2000) refutes the notion that common errors or misconceptions will be 'spread' among children through discussion: rather, she suggests that such activities will encourage children to review their thinking, leading to self-correction. Pound's research in Early Years settings supports this and found that peer discussion in play situations provided opportunities for rehearsing misconceptions. Through such rehearsals – providing that there were no interjections from adults – children develop better understandings as they *are able to challenge their own and other children's misconceptions* (Pound, 2008, page 70).

The value in listening to explanations and the reasoning of others is viewed not only in the benefits to the restructuring of the specific and immediate mathematical idea, but also in the overall contribution to the development of individual mathematical thinking. This would suggest that the skills involved in using logic, reasoning, communication and problem-solving – the very skills inherent in children's ability to use and apply mathematics – are actively developed by teaching beliefs and approaches which are deemed as *connectionist*.

Tanner and Jones (2000) suggest that restructuring thinking to accommodate new knowledge is not easy. In Piagetian terms this presents the children with *uncomfortable learning* as previously assimilated knowledge has to be revisited, reshaped and challenged. In order for this to happen the authors suggest that:

- children need to accept and appreciate that their response is *not quite right*;
- the learning process and environment need to be of sufficient importance to the children in order to make the effort to restructure and change their thinking;
- teachers need to accept that just explaining the misconception is not enough – the children will need help in the restructuring process.

The above is referred to as teaching for *cognitive conflict*: this describes children presented with examples and problems which lead to illogical outcomes. An example could be addition of fractions $\frac{1}{2} + \frac{1}{4}$ ...: if the strategy of 'add across top and bottom' is applied, this result ($\frac{2}{6}$) can be compared to a demonstration of a bar of chocolate where $\frac{1}{2}$ is given to pupil A and $\frac{1}{4}$ is given to pupil B – how much is left? ($\frac{1}{4}$). The two different answers to the same example create conflict between existing conceptual understanding (to add fractional values just 'add across') and new information which challenges this existing framework. This conflict can be resolved through peer discussion, sharing of ideas, justifying responses, listening to others and teacher questioning. *Accommodation* can only occur when restructuring takes place within one's schema to deal with this cognitive conflict.

Ryan and Williams (2007, page 13) argue that misconceptions are often *intelligent constructions that should be valued by learners and teachers alike* and as such suggest that what is needed is a *related teaching design or strategy that engages or conflicts with the underlying misconception and reasoning directly* (page 16).

Controlling mathematical dialogue in classrooms

Chapter 1 introduced the notion of the teacher mediating children's learning. Swan (2001, page 150) believes that mistakes and misconceptions *should be welcomed, made explicit, discussed and modified* if long-term learning is to take place. He suggests that this is unlikely to happen unless the teacher and children negotiate the *social nature of the classroom* and establish a classroom ethos based on trust, mutual support and value of individual viewpoints: there is a recognition that this is not easy and could result in teacher loss of confidence through apparent reduction in 'control', reduction in amount of 'work' produced on paper as more emphasis is placed on discussion, and noisier classrooms.

While some of this research was undertaken in junior-aged classes, it has to be acknowledged that the majority of research undertaken in this area has been with Key Stage 3 and Key Stage 4 children. The issue of a child's maturity level to be able to deal with conflicting points of view, or engage in mathematical dialogue, is an important one and may lead teachers in Foundation Stage settings and Key Stage 1 classrooms to believe such an approach 'unworkable'. It is interesting to note, however, that effective learning in mathematics appears to be connected with a school policy on an expectation that all children within the primary school will explain their mathematical ideas and methods (Askew *et al.*, 1997). The notion of provoking cognitive conflict is not alien to a young child's mathematical learning experiences: consider the 'conflict' caused by noticing that a 'small' object appears to be heavier than a 'big' object, a 'tall' container holds less water than a 'short' container or that the digit 4 can be 'worth' different amounts depending on the position of that digit in, for example, two- or three-digit numbers. The following chapters provide further discussion on this.

The development of a *learning culture* within classrooms is fundamental for teachers and children alike to explore how challenge can be an opportunity for new learning to take place. Hughes and Vass (2001) suggest that teacher language needs to be supportive in this respect: they identify the types of teacher language which would be helpful in supporting and motivating children to take risks in their learning. For example:

- the language of success – *I know you can*;
- the language of hope – *you can do it* and *what help do you need to do it?*;
- the language of possibility – supporting a climate of greater possibility by the choice of response comment – *yes, you did get it a bit mixed up but let's see which bit is causing you problems*.

Ryan and Williams (2007, page 27) take this further by suggesting that teachers and pupils should view themselves as belonging to a *community of enquiry* in which the notion of *persuasion with coherent reasoning* is the norm. In such a community pupils are encouraged to share responsibility for sustaining the dialogue.

A key factor appears to be the 'control' and use made of teacher/pupil and pupil/pupil mathematical dialogue. Effective teachers of numeracy (Askew et al., 1997) encourage both types of dialogue, allow it to be sustained, and use the results to help establish and emphasise connections and address misconceptions.

The role of questioning

Watson and Mason (1998, page 37) describe the learning of mathematics taking place within a *social situation of talk, comprising of discussion, questions, prompts and answers in which the teacher and children are as much a part of what mathematical activity is as what is in a textbook, on the worksheets, or on the board*. Teacher and/or child questioning is viewed as questioning to enhance and develop learning rather than questioning to see if the 'correct' answer has been achieved. While there is some need for the latter, if it becomes the focus for teacher questioning there is a danger that children will develop a model of mathematical behaviour which gives the responses they think acceptable; it avoids suggesting alternatives and hides queries/areas of confusion. Relying on answers alone, therefore, will not alert teachers to any underlying misconceptions. Worse still, simply correcting mathematical 'errors' without explanation, or engaging with reason, could lead to a pupil regarding mathematics as meaningless.

A Qualifications and Curriculum Authority (QCA) report into using assessment to raise achievement in mathematics (QCA, 2001) identified the need for teacher questioning to make greater use of *probing questions* to extend into dialogue which built upon pupil responses in order to elicit the child's thinking and develop the child's understanding further. Ofsted (2003) noted that one characteristic of mathematics lessons they deemed unsatisfactory was a tendency for teachers to do most of the talking. This resulted in children having *too few opportunities to try out their ideas orally, testing their thinking against that of others*. Where teachers used oral work well, they were more likely to:

- discover and deal with errors or misconceptions and adjust their teaching in the light of these;
- help children to reflect on and sort out ideas and confirm their own understanding.

(Ofsted, 2003, pages 18–19)

Listening to children's questions also provides opportunities to gain insights into levels of understanding, errors in use of terminology and underlying misconceptions. Providing children with a diet of closed questions or tasks is therefore unlikely to allow teachers to ascertain children's errors or misconceptions.

Skilful questioning can have the additional benefit of providing opportunities for children to engage in creative thinking and responses in mathematics (Briggs and Davis, 2008).

Reflection

The National Strategies placed emphasis on child interaction and participation, particularly in the whole-class elements of each lesson, and encouraged discussion and co-operation between children in group/paired work. The guidance provided recommended that teachers should use effective questioning techniques which allow children thinking time, encourage explanation of methods and reasoning, and probe reasons for incorrect answers. Much of the advice in this area focused on how best to develop mathematical language and reasoning through guided group work. Mathematical language was defined in the guidance as *not just vocabulary but children's ability to confidently explain their methods and solutions, choices, decisions and reasoning* and the guidance advocates *interaction and sustained discussion as opposed to a single question and moving on* (DfES, 2007, page 8).

However, Ofsted (2009, page 5) continues to report that in primary mathematics *most lessons do not emphasise mathematical talk enough; as a result, pupils struggle to express and develop their thinking* and that teachers *did not show enough urgency in checking whether each pupil had started the work correctly, had shown any of the expected misconceptions or was being challenged enough* (page 19) In contrast, they identify that *the best teachers focus on pupils' errors as a learning point. They spot the significant misconceptions which are illuminated by pupils' mistakes* (page 41).

Creating more time for reflection, dialogue, interpretations and assessment of errors and misconceptions would clearly lead to less mathematical 'content' being taught but, as research demonstrates, more deep-rooted, long-term mathematical learning taking place. Kafai and Harel (1991) refer to reflection as an *incubation phase* and Ackermann (1991) identifies a *cognitive dance* where children necessarily 'dive in' and 'step back' from a situation to create balance and understanding. Freudenthal (1991, page 127) explains how reflection is an integral part of children *expanding their reality* or *expanding common sense*. Similarly, Ackermann (1991) believes that children's mathematical development is achieved through the *progressive widening of fields of experience* and Pratt and Noss (2002) refer to the *broadening of contextual neighbourhood*. However it is referred to, it appears that reflection enables the development of children's mathematical understanding.

Implications for planning

Misconceptions are a natural outcome of intelligent mathematical development involving con-nections, generalisations, and concept formation ... they signal a learning opportunity or zone and so, potential for development – for example – through targeted teaching

(Ryan and Williams, 2007, page 270)

It appears that effective teaching of mathematics involves planning to expose and discuss errors and misconceptions in such a way that children are challenged to think, encouraged to ask questions and listen to explanations, and helped to reflect upon these experiences. This suggests that the more aware teachers and trainee teachers are of the common errors and possible misconceptions associated with a topic, the more effective will be the planning to address and deal with such.

Ofsted (2009, page 4) identify that a good teacher of mathematics recognises *quickly when pupils already understand the work or what their misconception might be. They extend thinking through building on pupils' contributions, questions and misconceptions to aid learning, flexibly adapting to meet needs and confidently departing from plans.*

The role of questioning, dialogue and discussion is significant if children are to shift their perspectives on only contributing if they think they have a 'correct' answer, or the answer they believe is wanted by their teacher.

Swan (2003, pages 119–122) discusses types of activities which are helpful to generate dis-cussions likely to uncover children's misconceptions: the use of cards which have equiva-lent representations of the same concept, or statement cards which have to be sorted as always true, never true or sometimes true, place children in situations where choices have to be justified or counter-examples provided.

It seems that a growing emphasis on children participating in meaningful mathematical dialogue which assists in the exposure of 'alternative' constructions has implications for the amount of time teachers should plan to teach new content.

Summary

The research demonstrates that teaching to avoid children developing misconceptions is unhelpful and could result in misconceptions being hidden from the teacher (and from themselves).

There needs to be a greater recognition from teachers that mathematical misconceptions are much more deep rooted than errors and that it takes time for children and other learn-ers to resolve long-held misconceptions. This implies that a shift in the mindset is needed for teachers to move from planning mathematical lessons to avoid errors/misconceptions occurring, to actively planning lessons which will confront children with carefully chosen examples which will allow for challenge, dialogue and restructuring of thinking.

Misconceptions are a natural part of a child's conceptual development and consequent-ly, greater time in mathematical lessons should be given to encourage children to make connections between aspects of mathematical learning and their own meanings. The time needed for children's reflection, examination of their own ideas, and comparison with those of other children and the mathematical situation presented, challenges the amount of mathematical content often covered in primary schools. The amount of time spent on revision for the National Tests continues to distort the curriculum (Ofsted, 2009) and is unhelpful in encouraging all teachers of mathematics to adopt teaching practices which would focus more on exploring and diagnosing misconceptions.

Regardless of the time allocated to mathematical discussion or activity, the culture of the classroom has to be one in which children are 'rewarded' for having the courage to test out their mathematical ideas in order for errors and misconceptions to be aired, discussed and resolved. If getting the right answer is the aim of the activity, or presenting the work in a neat way, or completing a set of exercises in a given time, then probing children's misunderstandings and misconceptions may prove difficult and counter-productive to effective mathematical learning.

Numbers and the number system

Fiona Lawton and Alice Hansen

Chapter overview

Children spend a considerable amount of curriculum time engaging in activities related to number. The size of Chapters 3 and 4 reflects the centrality of number in the primary school mathematics curriculum. Many number concepts are taught in a hierarchical sequence because the ability to understand and engage with more difficult concepts relies upon a sound understanding of ideas met earlier in the curriculum. Place value, for example, underpins much of the number curriculum, as does counting. Teachers therefore might consider how the use of a spiral curriculum (Bruner, 1960; see also Chapter 1) may support the teaching and learning of number in the primary curriculum. In the Early Years Foundation Stage (DCSF, 2007, page 14) children are expected to be *supported in developing their understanding of problem solving, reasoning and numeracy in a broad range of contexts in which they can explore, enjoy, learn, practise and talk about their developing understanding.* Number forms Attainment Target 2 of the National Curriculum for Mathematics in England (DfEE, 1999b). In Key Stage 1 children develop an understanding of whole numbers and using informal calculation strategies for the four rules of arithmetic. Throughout Key Stage 2, the concept of number is broadened to include fractions, decimals and percentages. Algebraic ideas are embedded within the number Programme of Study for mathematics at both Key Stage 1 and Key Stage 2.

Counting

Counting is one of the earlier mathematical concepts that children learn. Children learn to count both formally and informally through interaction with others and their environment. Amazingly, by six years of age, the average child attending an educational setting has an understanding of number which took man several thousands of years to discover. Dauben and Scriba (2002) explore the development of counting systems in great detail. Our decimal system has only developed over the last 5000 years and there are still places in the world today where the indigenous population cannot count beyond two. Interestingly, seminal research undertaken by American psychologists Gelman and Gallistel shows that learning to count mirrors the historical development of counting. Gelman and Gallistel (1986, 2004) spent six years researching children's cognitive development in number and formulated five principles of counting. These principles are outlined below.

The Gelman and Gallistel 'how-to-count' principles

The one-one principle – a child understanding the one-one principle understands that each item to be counted has a name and that we only count each item once during the counting process. The child needs to make a physical or mental *tag* of the items to be counted and the counted items and keep them separate.

The stable-order principle – a child understanding the stable-order principle knows that every time we use number names to count a set of items, the order of the number names does not change. In English the order of the number names is always one, two, three, four, etc., **every** time a set of objects is counted.

The cardinal principle – a child understanding the cardinal principle knows the answer to 'how many?' The child knows that the last number counted represents the number of items in the set of objects.

The abstraction principle – a child understanding the abstraction principle knows that 'anything' can be counted and that not all the 'anythings' need to be of the same type.

The order-irrelevance principle – a child understanding the order-irrelevance principle knows that we can start to count with any object in a set of objects; we don't have to count from left to right, for example (adapted from Gelman and Gallistel, 1986, pages 77–83).

The importance placed on the findings of Gelman and Gallistel is reflected in the Early Years Foundation Stage Statutory Framework (DfEE, 2007) where it is possible to find the *'how-to-count'* principles embedded.

In Key Stage 1 children are expected to understand all the *how-to-count* principles. Munn (2008) describes the typical responses of young children to a range of counting activities and she describes what a typical child understands at particular ages. Munn researched children's beliefs about counting and found *preschool children appear to have little or no understanding of the adult purpose of counting* (page 17). The interesting point about Munn's research is that the children believed they **could** count because they understood counting as saying the words in the right order. No doubt readers have heard friends and relatives boasting that their child could count at only three years old. Teachers need to be aware that children who can apparently count fluently may, in fact, just be 'reeling off' the number names by rote. The danger here is that the child might be introduced to more complex concepts before s/he understands what is meant by counting.

Since counting underpins early arithmetic concepts (Donlan, 2003), it is important that teachers are able to provide appropriate counting activities to support a child's learning. Having an awareness of the *how-to-count* principles will enable practitioners to understand the nature of counting and the potential difficulties that children may face during their journey to successful counting.

You can read more about how counting develops into the four rules of arithmetic in Chapter 4.

3.1 Consistent counting

The teacher asks the children how many teddies altogether have come to the picnic (see Figure 3.1).

Figure 3.1: One child says, One, two, three, four, six, nine, ten.

The errors

The child has made two errors. He has counted one teddy twice and he has omitted *five*, *seven* and *eight* in his counting sequence.

Why this happens

The child's first error has occurred because he does not understand the one–one principle. He has 'counted' one of the bears twice. This may be because he cannot remember which teddy he 'counted' first. The child is unable to separate the 'counted' objects from the 'to be counted' objects. The child's second error is that he is unfamiliar with the counting sequence. He does not understand the stable-order principle. He knows by heart the number sequence, *one*, *two*, *three*, *four*, but then chooses any number he has 'heard' for the rest of the sequence. Children need to know the English counting sequence before they can count effectively.

Curriculum links		
EYFS	Say and use number names in order in familiar contexts	
EYFS	Count reliably up to ten everyday objects	
KS1	Ma2 2a	Count reliably up to 20 objects at first and recognise that if the objects are rearranged the number stays the same

3.2 Abstraction and order irrelevance

The teacher asks a child how many things he has collected altogether (Figure 3.2). He is hesitant. The teacher knows that the child can count up to ten buttons or cars without any difficulty in the nursery. She asks him again. He empties out his bucket and groups his pinecones, rocks and leaves.

Figure 3.2

The error

The child has not counted all the objects together and therefore cannot find the total.

Why this happens

The child is not using the abstraction principle. He does not understand that we can count a mixed set of objects. He thinks that all the objects have to be of the same type or class. Another possible reason for the child's hesitation is that he is unable to understand the order-irrelevance principle and so could only count the objects when they were laid out in a line. The child, at this stage, needs to count the objects from one side to another, he doesn't realise that we can start the count with any object. His decision to lay out the objects in a line may also be related to difficulties with partitioning the 'counted' and 'to be counted' objects in an irregular array.

Curriculum links		
EYFS	Count reliably up to ten everyday objects	
EYFS	Begin to relate addition to combining two groups of objects and subtraction to 'taking away'	
KS1	Ma2 2a	Count reliably up to 20 objects at first and recognise that if the objects are rearranged the number stays the same

3.3 Conservation of number: More or less?

The teacher asks a child to look at two groups of counters and tell her which one contains more (see Figure 3.3). She states that the group with four large counters has more than the group with six small counters.

Figure 3.3

The error

The child has used a visual cue to deem that the group with four large counters has more than the group with six small counters.

Why this happens

Visual cues are often more convincing than other cues. The child may have even counted the objects in both sets and known that there were six and four respectively, but because the four counters take up more area, this has an overriding impact on the child's understanding of knowing the total number of counters in each group. This is known as conservation, a notion introduced by Piaget.

Curriculum links		
EYFS	Count reliably up to ten everyday objects	
EYFS	Use language such as 'more' or 'less' to compare two numbers	
EYFS	Use language such as 'greater', 'smaller', 'heavier' or 'lighter' to compare quantities	
KS1	Ma2 1e	Use the correct language, symbols and vocabulary associated with number and data
KS1	Ma2 2a	Count reliably up to 20 objects at first and recognise that if the objects are rearranged the number stays the same

Place value

The term 'place value' is used to describe the method by which numbers are represented in written form. The modern place-value system is based on the Hindu-Arabic method, which only became consistently used in Europe from the fifteenth century. The Hindu-Arabic system is a pure place-value system which is the most effective method of representing numbers, particularly if we wish to perform calculations with them. Given that it took such a long time to develop the modern place-value system, it is not surprising that many children find place-value concepts difficult. There are several underpinning structures to place value which children need to understand if they are to progress from counting, to representing numbers, to written calculations. The key principles are given below.

Digits – there are only ten digits in the system (0, 1, 2, 3, 4, 5, 6, 7, 8 and 9).

Position – the columnar position of a digit determines its value.

Base 10 – in our system we use base 10. Columns represent increasing/decreasing powers of 10.

Zero – we use zero to represent an empty column (0 as a place holder).

Grouping and exchange – once we have ten objects in a column, we can exchange them for one object in the next column to the left and vice versa.

If we stop to consider that there are so many principles to learn and understand, it enables us to reflect upon the challenges that this presents for children. The first obstacle faced by young children is that numerals are abstract concepts. When children learn to count, they usually do so by being introduced to concrete objects that can be moved, touched and seen. Numerals themselves bear no relation to the objects with which children are familiar. Baroody *et al.* (2006) discuss Ginsburg's work that began in the 1970s. They identify how a key source of learning difficulties is the gap between children's existing knowledge and the teaching they receive at school. There are two main causes for this gap. These are: (a) *unconnected formal instruction*, and (b) *spotty or inadequate informal knowledge* (page 198). Others, such as Dickson *et al.* (1984, page 206) also use Ginsburg's (1977) seminal work. They explain how Ginsburg suggested that there are three stages to understanding place value.

Stage 1 – the child can write a number correctly but cannot explain why.

Stage 2 – the child can recognise when a number has been written down incorrectly.

Stage 3 – the child can understand what each digit in a number represents.

In summary, the teaching and learning of mathematics that depends on understanding place value is complex. To support children, teachers need to be able to accurately diagnose children's place value errors. They should not attempt to re-teach poorly understood methods, but return to earlier stages of understanding of place-value concepts.

You can read further about how place value supports calculation in Chapter 4.

3.4 The names of written numerals

The error

The child has reversed the digits in the number (see Figure 3.4).

Figure 3.4

Why this happens

The child has written the numeral 4 first because in the English counting system we say *'four*teen'. The teens numbers often cause this difficulty. In addition, for 11 and 12, children must learn two new number names.

Curriculum links		
EYFS	Recognise numerals 1 to 9	
KS1	Ma2 1e	Use the correct language, symbols and vocabulary associated with number and data
KS1	Ma2 1f	Communicate in spoken, pictorial and written form, at first using informal language and recording, then mathematical language and symbols
KS1	Ma2 2c	Read and write numbers to 20 at first and then to 100 or beyond; understand and use the vocabulary of comparing and ordering these numbers; recognise that the position of a digit gives its value and know what each digit represents, including zero as a place holder; order a set of one- and two-digit numbers and position them on a number line and hundred-square; round any two-digit number to the nearest 10
KS2	Ma2 2c	Read, write and order whole numbers, recognising that the position of a digit gives its value

3.5 Using 'digit' and 'number'

A teacher overhears a child in his class saying to his friend, *Write down the number 6 and the number 3. That makes sixty-three.*

The error

The child is using the term 'number' incorrectly. In this situation, the number contains two digits.

Why this happens

Perhaps the child has heard others saying that four add two make six and he has borrowed some of the language to explain to his friend how to write 63. He has understood that four and six are numbers, but he has just to understand that 0, 1, 2, 3, 4, 5, 6, 7, 8 and 9 should be referred to as digits when they are used in numerals. So, 5 is a one-digit number, written using the digit '5', and '5' is also a numeral. 327 is a three-digit number, written using the digits '3', '2' and '7'. It is a numeral, where the digit '2' in the tens column has a value of 20.

Curriculum links		
KS1	Ma2 1e	Use the correct language, symbols and vocabulary associated with number and data
KS1	Ma2 1f	Communicate in spoken, pictorial and written form, at first using informal language and recording, then mathematical language and symbols
KS2	Ma2 1i	Communicate mathematically, including the use of precise mathematical language

3.6 Reading and writing whole numbers

The teacher writes the number **609** on the board and asks the children to say the number (Figure 3.5). A child says it is the number sixty-nine.

That is the number sixty-nine!

Figure 3.5

The error

The child has read the digits as 60 and 9. The child does not recognise that the 6 is worth 6 hundreds (600) because it is in the hundreds column.

Why this happens

This type of error occurs because the child does not understand that the position of a digit determines its value. The child may be unaware of the principles of grouping and exchange. Children need to have practical experience of grouping sets of objects into tens and then exchanging each group of ten for another object which represents a 'ten' and so on for hundreds, thousands, etc.

Conversely, when asked to write **'six hundred and nine'**, a child may write **'6009'**, i.e. 600 and (then) 9. Again this error occurs because the child does not understand that the position of a digit determines its value and they write what they hear.

Curriculum links		
KS1	Ma2 1e	Use the correct language, symbols and vocabulary associated with number and data
KS1	Ma2 1f	Communicate in spoken, pictorial and written form, at first using informal language and recording, then mathematical language and symbols

KS1	Ma2 2c	Read and write numbers to 20 at first and then to 100 or beyond; understand and use the vocabulary of comparing and ordering these numbers; recognise that the position of a digit gives its value and know what each digit represents, including zero as a place holder; order a set of one- and two-digit numbers and position them on a number line and hundred-square; round any two-digit number to the nearest 10
KS2	Ma2 2c	Read, write and order whole numbers, recognising that the position of a digit gives its value

3.7 The concept of zero as a place holder

Children are working with multi-base 10 apparatus. A child has a number of items on her table (Figure 3.6). The child is asked by the teacher to record the number represented by the apparatus.

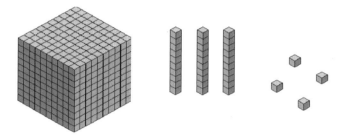

Figure 3.6: A child says 'one thousand and thirty four' but writes: 134.

The error

The child does not understand the need to use zero as a place holder.

Why this happens

The child does not understand that if we have no 'hundreds' we must write 0 in the hundreds column so that the recorded digits are given in the correct position, i.e. the 1 in the thousands position, the 3 in the tens position and the 4 in the units position. This error may have occurred because the child does not understand that the position of a digit determines its value.

A similar example of the confusion surrounding the use of zero is the case where a child believes that 0.6 is smaller than 0.600. Here the child does not understand that the zeros in the hundredths and thousandths positions have no significance.

Curriculum links		
KS1	Ma2 1e	Use the correct language, symbols and vocabulary associated with number and data
KS1	Ma2 1f	Communicate in spoken, pictorial and written form, at first using informal language and recording, then mathematical language and symbols
KS1	Ma2 2c	Read and write numbers to 20 at first and then to 100 or beyond; understand and use the vocabulary of comparing and ordering these numbers; recognise that the position of a digit gives its value and know what each digit represents, including zero as a place holder; order a set of one- and two-digit numbers and position them on a number line and hundred square; round any two-digit number to the nearest 10
KS2	Ma2 2c	Read, write and order whole numbers, recognising that the position of a digit gives its value

3.8 Reading and ordering decimal numbers

The teacher writes two numbers on the whiteboard (see Figure 3.7). The children are asked to discuss and then identify the largest number. One group claim that 8.35 is the largest number.

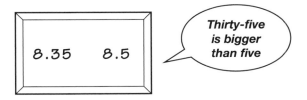

Figure 3.7

The error

When asked why, the group says that 8.35 is larger because 35 is larger than 5 so 8.35 must be larger than 8.5.

Why this happens

The group have read the digits after the decimal point as if they were whole numbers. They may have read the numbers as 'eight point thirty five' and 'eight point five' respectively. They do not understand the relative value of successive groupings of ten in the place-value system for numbers to the right of the decimal point. They need to know that for each place to the right of the decimal point, the numbers are successively smaller by powers of ten. Additionally, some children believe that numbers are larger if there are more decimal digits. Teachers should ensure that children correctly name decimals to help to overcome this difficulty, i.e. 'eight point three five' and 'eight point five'. This type of error may occur because children have been using money as a context for decimals. In money it is quite legitimate to say 'eight, thirty-five'. This is a potential drawback of the use of money to explore the concept of decimals.

Curriculum links		
KS1	Ma2 2c	Read and write numbers to 20 at first and then to 100 or beyond; understand and use the vocabulary of comparing and ordering these numbers; recognise that the position of a digit gives its value and know what each digit represents, including zero as a place holder; order a set of one- and two-digit numbers and position them on a number line and hundred square; round any two-digit number to the nearest 10

Money

Given the recent and ongoing international financial context we are faced with, introducing how to manage money into education is a growing concern in a number of countries (e.g. National Institute for Budget Advice, 2009; Personal Finance Education Group, 2010). Teachers need to consider if the money problems that they present to children do encourage them to make decisions.

Increased use of bank cards is reducing children's opportunities to observe money being handled, so it is crucially important that teachers introduce children to 'real' money in the classroom so that children can learn the currency. *Mummy, why is the shopkeeper paying you for your shopping?* This classic misconception is common among young children. It occurs when the parent or carer hands over a note and is given several coins change. The child may simply 'see' the coins and notes as objects and is drawing his knowledge of number concepts to frame his question. Furthermore, Cole (2009) reflects on how the increasingly cashless society is impacting on children's understanding of money:

> There was a time, not so long ago, when the obligation to pay hard cash for school dinners, bus fares and weekly Brownie subs brought money into a child's life gently and naturally. Now parents are more than likely to pay for these things by direct debit, and primary school children are much more likely to be ferried around by car than to take a bus. When public transport does become part of growing up, cashless Oyster cards are likely to give them their ticket to ride. When I was a young lad my mum gave me a couple of 2p coins for my secret inside pocket in case I needed to use a phone box. My 11-year-old daughter, in contrast, has a (cheap) mobile phone that I bought her, topped up with credits buzzed over from my branchless bank account.

Dickson *et al.* (1984) explain that Gibson (1981) identified three key ideas that children need to understand money.

Coin recognition – children need to be able to identify all the coins and notes in the currency.
Equivalence – children need to know that two 5-pence coins are the same as one 10-pence coin.

Practical situations – children need to be able to make decisions relating to buying and selling.

Keat and Wilburne (2009) explored the impact of using story books on young children's ability to recognise and use coins. They found that using children's literature encouraged the children to set and solve their own problems, reason answers, and correctly identify the value of coins. The children had previously been unable to do this through more 'traditional' styles of teaching.

You can read further about using money in number operations and calculation in Chapter 4.

3.9 The value of money

A child is shown the following coins by his teacher (Figure 3.8). The teacher asks him how much money he has. He says he has four pennies.

Figure 3.8

The error

The child has counted the number of coins instead of finding the total value of the coins.

Why this happens

The child does not understand that coins have value. He has counted the coins as if they were objects. This error is common with young children because they may still be learning to count. They may just be reaching the stage where they can understand the concept of cardinality, so do not understand the idea of items having a numerical value more than one. Refer to the 'Counting' section for an explanation of how children learn to count.

Curriculum links		
EYFS	Use developing mathematical ideas and methods to solve problems	
KS1	Ma2 4a	Choose sensible calculation methods to solve whole-number problems (including problems involving money or measures), drawing on their understanding of the operations

3.10 The relative value of money

The teacher asks a child which of the coins in Figure 3.9 is worth the most. She points to the 2-pence piece and says this coin is worth the most.

Figure 3.9

The error

The child has identified the wrong coin.

Why this happens

The child believes that the bigger the object, the more it is worth. She may believe this because of her experiences in relation to measures, where generally the bigger an object is, the more numerical value can be attributed to it. The child does not understand that the value of a coin is not directly proportional to its size.

The above child does not understand the concept of equivalence and may also have a limited knowledge of currency. Teachers need to ensure that children have considerable opportunities to handle 'real' money in role-play contexts before moving on to more complex and, essentially abstract, pencil and paper money problems.

Curriculum links		
KS1	Ma2 4a	Choose sensible calculation methods to solve whole-number problems (including problems involving money or measures), drawing on their understanding of the operations

3.11 Representing money on a calculator

A child has used a calculator to help solve a problem involving money. The calculator states that the answer is 1.5, so she writes £1.5 and says *One pound and five pence.*

The error

There are two errors made by the child here: (1) She has incorrectly written the answer of £1.50 as £1.5; (2) she has read 1.5 on the calculator as 'One pound and five pence' rather than 'One pound and fifty pence'.

Why this happens

The child may not know that the calculator automatically displays a truncated answer of 1.50 to 1.5 on the display. Alternatively, she may not have taken into consideration the context of the answer. She has not considered that an answer of 1.5 means 1.5 (or 1½) pounds in this case, which is written as one pound and fifty pence: £1.50. It could also be that she has not used zero as a place holder, but reads the answer as one pound and fifty pence (thus ignoring the zero in the hundreds column) or as one pound and five pence (thus ignoring the need for a zero in the tenths column).

Curriculum links

KS2	Ma2 1h	Present and interpret solutions in the context of the problem
KS2	Ma2 2i	Understand and use decimal notation for tenths and hundredths in context
KS2	Ma2 3k	Use a calculator for calculations involving several digits, including decimals; use a calculator to solve number problems; know how to enter and interpret money calculations and fractions

Fractions

It is a requirement of the National Curriculum that children meet fractions formally in Key Stage 2, although a lot of teachers will have introduced them earlier than this. It is important to remember that most children will have met fractions informally in an everyday context and teachers need to be aware of the potential for misconceptions arising from these encounters. For example, a parent may encourage a child to choose the 'biggest half' of a food item they are sharing. However, this is incorrect as mathematically, the halves should be equal.

Lamon (2001) argues that *traditional instruction in fractions does not encourage meaningful performance* (page 146). She researched the effect of teaching fractions for understanding and found that where learning was underpinned by understanding, children were able to solve problems involving more complex fractions. Similarly, Critchley (2002) describes how a *real* problem-solving activity involving the use of fractions supported a child's ability to understand and use them.

There are many different interpretations of fractions and it is important that teachers are both aware of and understand these interpretations so they can introduce them to children in a meaningful way. Teachers also need to be aware that some interpretations of fractions are conceptually more difficult than others. The relative conceptual difficulty of particular interpretations of fractions is widely recognised by mathematics educators (Charalambous and Pitta-Pantazi, 2005).

- **Part of a whole** – here an object is 'split' into two or more equal parts.
- **Part of a set of objects** – what part of the set of objects has a particular characteristic?
- **Number on a number line** – numbers which are represented *between* whole numbers.
- **Operator** – the result of a division.
- **Ratio** – comparing the relative size of two objects or sets of objects.

The first interpretation in this list is that a fraction is part of a whole. Charalambous and Pitta-Pantazi's (2005) research identified that while this way of teaching fractions was necessary, it was not appropriate to use this as the only way in to teaching the other interpretations of fractions. They explained how it was necessary that *teachers need to scaffold students to develop a profound understanding of the different interpretations of fractions, since such an understanding could also offer to uplift students' performance in tasks related to the operations of fractions* (Charalambous and Pitta-Pantazi, 2005, page 239).

You can read further about calculating with fractions in Chapter 4.

3.12 Fractions as part of a shape

The teacher asks the children to divide a semicircle into quarters. One child's response is given in Figure 3.10.

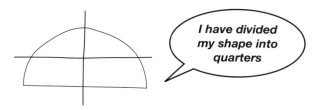

Figure 3.10

The error

The child has not divided the semicircle into four equal parts.

Why this happens

The child does not understand that all the parts must be equal. He may not have had sufficient experience of dividing physical objects into equal parts where the parts can be directly compared to each other. Additionally, he may be used to dividing squares, oblongs and circles so he thinks the methods he has used for these shapes works for all shapes. In effect, he incorrectly generalises the methods he has used for squares, oblongs and circles.

Curriculum links

KS2	Ma2 2d	Understand unit fractions then fractions that are several parts of one whole, locate them on a number line and use them to find fractions of shapes and quantities
KS2	Ma2 2g	Recognise approximate proportions of a whole and use simple fractions and percentages to describe them, explaining their methods and reasoning

3.13 Fractions as part of a set of objects

The teacher asks two children what fraction of the set in Figure 3.11 is black. They say one-third.

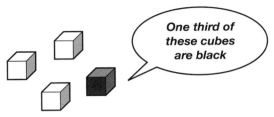

One third of these cubes are black

Figure 3.11

The error

The children have failed to take the complete set of objects as the whole unit.

Why this happens

The children have compared the one black cube against the three white cubes and concluded that one-third of the set of objects is black. This misconception may be common in children up to about seven years of age and may be related to Piaget's findings from his class-inclusion task. Piaget found that if children are presented with a set of say five red objects and two blue objects and asked if there are more red objects or more 'objects', children will say there are more red objects. This is because they compare the red objects with the blue objects instead of comparing the red objects with the total number of objects in the set.

Curriculum links		
KS2	Ma2 2d	Understand unit fractions then fractions that are several parts of one whole, locate them on a number line and use them to find fractions of shapes and quantities
KS2	Ma2 2g	Recognise approximate proportions of a whole and use simple fractions and percentages to describe them, explaining their methods and reasoning

3.14 Fractions as numbers on a number line

The teacher is using a counting stick in the oral/mental part of the daily mathematics lesson (Figure 3.12). She tells children that one end of the counting stick represents 0 and the other end of the counting stick represents 10. She asks one child to place '½' on the counting stick. He places his card in the centre of the counting stick.

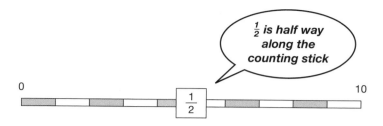

Figure 3.12

The error

The child has placed his card halfway along the counting stick instead of halfway between 0 and 1.

Why this happens

When children are introduced to fractions they are introduced to unit fractions such as one-half or one-quarter. They sometimes believe that a fraction is a number smaller than one, i.e. between 0 and 1. Children can usually successfully identify fractions on a number line between 0 and 1. The difficulty arises when the number line is extended to include numbers greater than 1.

Curriculum links		
KS2	Ma2 2d	Understand unit fractions then fractions that are several parts of one whole, locate them on a number line and use them to find fractions of shapes and quantities

3.15 Naming fractions

Two children are working with their teacher shading in parts of shapes (see Figure 3.13). The teacher asks them what fraction of the shape has been shaded. One of them tells the teacher that one-'twoth' of the shape has been shaded.

Figure 3.13

The error

The child is trying to apply a consistent naming system to a system which is not fully consistent.

Why this happens

The child is actually thinking logically. Furani (2003) explores how naming and misnaming involve logic and rules, and are often an aid to supporting their mathematical learning. Unfortunately, there are inconsistencies in the English conventions of naming fractions and this can confuse children. Indeed, in American English, one-quarter is referred to as 'one fourth'. The child needs to learn that we use the term 'half' to represent 1 out of 2. Another common error with naming fractions is the use of 'one whole'. Sometimes children interpret this as 'one hole'.

Curriculum links		
KS1	Ma2 1e	Use the correct language, symbols and vocabulary associated with number and data
KS2	Ma2 1i	Communicate mathematically, including the use of precise mathematical language
KS2	Ma2 2d	Understand unit fractions then fractions that are several parts of one whole, locate them on a number line and use them to find fractions of shapes and quantities

3.16 Writing fractions

The children have been given some cards with unit fractions written on them (Figure 3.14). The teacher asks the children to look at the two cards below and say which is the biggest.

Figure 3.14

The error

The child believes that one-third is bigger than one-half because the denominator of one-third is larger than the denominator of one-half.

Why this happens

The child is using his knowledge of whole numbers to order the fractions. He is over-generalising whole-number concepts. The child does not understand the written notation of fractions. He needs to know what the notation means – that we have one part **out of** three equal parts. The child probably does not have a clear understanding of the concept of fractions in a practical sense.

Associated with this idea, children also need to realise that 'the line' in a fraction represents division. So means 3 **out of** 4, which is also 3 **divided by** 4.

Curriculum links		
KS2	Ma2 2d	Understand unit fractions then fractions that are several parts of one whole, locate them on a number line and use them to find fractions of shapes and quantities

Decimals

Decimal numbers are an extension of the whole-number place-value system. Bailey and Borwein (2010) argue that the modern system of decimal notation with zero, together with basic computational schemes, was the greatest discovery in mathematics. This happened over 1500 years ago in India, around 500 BC.

Decimal numbers are symbolic representations of units less than one (rational numbers) in the same way that the whole-number place-value system represents quantities of objects. The conceptual ideas underpinning decimals are the same as those underpinning fractions, for example part of a whole, part of a set, and so on (see discussion in 'Fraction' section above). In effect, decimals are simply another way of representing fractions in written form. The implication of this is that children need to have a sound understanding of fractions in order to use abstract decimal notation to represent fractions. Pagni (2004) argues that fractions and decimals should not be taught separately. Since fractions and decimals are representations for the same numbers, Pagni suggests teachers should show the connection between them by placing equivalent fractions and decimals on a number line.

Errors in the use of decimals are likely to have two sources of misunderstanding: place value and fractions (Moloney and Stacey, 1997). Where such errors occur, teachers might consider returning to much earlier concepts to ensure the child has sufficient understanding of these ideas to be able to use decimal notation.

3.17 Reading and writing decimals

The children are planning how to spend some additional school funds for their classroom. One group decides they want to buy a new carpet for the carpet area of their classroom.

The children measure and then calculate the area of the carpet area. It is 12 square metres. Their calculations are shown in Figure 3.15.

The error

The group have read 8.99 as 899.

We calculated the carpet would cost £10,788

Because the carpet cost £8.99 per metre

The area to be covered it is $12m^2$

So 12 × 899   is   10 × 899 + 2 × 899
                                8990   +   1798

                                      10,788

Figure 3.15

Why this happens

The children do not understand the significance of the decimal point in the place value system. This error is linked to the children's understanding of place value. The children do not understand what each digit in the number 8.99 represents; that we have £8 and 99 hundredths of a pound. Of course, this error might be simply a careless slip, but they have not used estimation strategies in order to consider the reasonableness of their answer.

Curriculum links		
KS2	Ma2 1a	Make connections in mathematics and appreciate the need to use numerical skills and knowledge when solving problems in other parts of the mathematics curriculum
KS2	Ma2 1e	Make mental estimates of the answers to calculations; check results
KS2	Ma2 1g	Use notation diagrams and symbols correctly within a given problem
KS2	Ma2 2i	Understand and use decimal notation for tenths and hundredths in context
KS2	Ma2 3j	Use written methods for short multiplication and division by a single-digit integer of two-digit then three-digit then four-digit integers, then of numbers with decimals; then use long multiplication, at first for two-digit by two-digit integer calculations, then for three-digit by two-digit calculations; extend division to informal methods of dividing by a two-digit divisor; use approximations and other strategies to check that their answers are reasonable
KS2	Ma2 4a	Choose, use and combine any of the four number operations to solve word problems involving numbers in real life, money or measures of length, mass, capacity or time, then perimeter and area

3.18 Ordering decimals

The teacher writes the following numbers on the board and asks the children to place them in order from smallest to largest: 0.15, 1.3, 0.095, 2.8 (see Figure 3.16).

A child writes the following on her whiteboard:

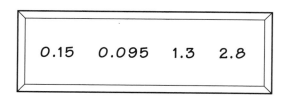

Figure 3.16

The error

The child thinks that 0.095 is larger than 0.15.

Why this happens

The child knows that 2.8 is bigger than 1.3 because she knows that 2 is larger than 1 from her understanding of whole numbers. However, when comparing two decimal numbers between 0 and 1, she does not understand which digit is most significant. She does not realise she must look to the tenths column first then to the hundredths column and finally to the thousandths column. The child does not have a clear understanding of the decimal place-value system. The child may also have read the numbers as 'nought point fifteen' and 'nought point ninety-five' and concluded that since 95 is larger than 15, that 0.095 is larger than 0.15. (See also place-value sections in this chapter and Chapter 4.)

Curriculum links		
KS2	Ma2 2i	Understand and use decimal notation for tenths and hundredths in context

3.19 Decimal systems and non-decimal systems

A class is going on a day trip to London. Two children use an internet site to check how long it will take them to get from Birmingham to London on the train (see Table 3.1).

They calculate that regardless of which train they get, the duration of the train journey will be the same: 1:24.

When the teacher asks them how long the journey will take, they say it will take *one point two four hours*.

Leaving	From	To	Arriving
08:10	Birmingham New Street [BHM]	London Euston [EUS]	09:34
08:30	Birmingham New Street [BHM]	London Euston [EUS]	09:54
08:50	Birmingham New Street [BHM]	London Euston [EUS]	10:14
09:10	Birmingham New Street [BHM]	London Euston [EUS]	10:34
09:30	Birmingham New Street [BHM]	London Euston [EUS]	10:54

Table 3.1 Train timetable

The error

The children have interpreted their answer as if it were a decimal rather than a length of time.

Why this happens

The children have completed their calculation using an algorithm for base-10 numbers and so they have interpreted their answer in base 10. They have not realised that their answer means 1 hour 24 minutes rather than 1.24 (one point two four) hours.

Curriculum links		
KS2	Ma2 1h	Present and interpret solutions in the context of the problem
KS2	Ma3 4d	Read the time from analogue and digital 12- and 24-hour clocks; use units of time – seconds, minutes, hours, days, weeks – and know the relationship between them

Percentages

The term 'per cent' means literally 'for every hundred'. Percentages are conceptually equivalent to the part-of-a-set interpretation of fractions – if our set contains 100 objects then we can easily see that if 50 of the objects have a particular attribute then 50 per cent (%) of the set can be said to have the attribute. Equally, we can relate percentages to the part–whole representation of fractions in that 'the whole' represents 100%. Percentages are used widely in 'everyday' life and children will have an understanding that 30% off in the sale means that the item is reduced in price. This does not mean that children understand the mathematics of percentages, similar to the way a young child who can 'reel off' the numbers to 20 can count (see 'Counting'). Like decimals, percentages are a method of representing rational numbers, so children need to have a sound understanding of fractions before being formally introduced to percentages.

In primary school, the focus should be helping children to understand the notion of **per cent** and relating this to simple fractional amounts, for example halves, quarters and tenths. It is tempting to think that we might introduce children to a mathematical formula in order to solve more complex percentage problems, but this should be avoided – it might be argued that teaching in this way leads to weak understanding and negative attitudes towards percentages. Instead, just as reported earlier in the 'Decimals' section, it is useful to introduce equivalent fractions, decimals and percentages together. Van den Heuvel-Panhuizen (2003) explores a Dutch Realistic Mathematics Education (RME) learning trajectory where Grade 5 children were taught percentages in a way that was *remarkable how easily the children got to work so easily … everything happened very naturally, and it was clear from the way in which the children discussed … that they knew what the percentages represented* (page 20) through a process drawing on the children's own experiences of using percentages, decimals and fractions.

To read about calculating percentages, see Chapter 4.

3.20 Equivalence of percentages, fractions and decimals

The teacher asks her class to colour in 50 squares in a 100 square. She tells the children that they have coloured in 50% of the 100 square. She asks the children what they notice. They children appear to grasp the idea that one half of the square has been coloured in. Mrs Smith then asks the children to colour in 25 squares of the 100 squares and is again pleased to note that the children seem to understand that 25% is the same as one-quarter. The following day she extends the activity. This time she asks the children to colour in 50% of a different number square. One child's response to the task is shown in Figure 3.17.

1	2	3	4	5	6	7	8	9	10
11	12	13	14	15	16	17	18	19	20
21	22	23	24	25	26	27	28	29	30
31	32	33	34	35	36	37	38	39	40
41	42	43	44	45	46	47	48	49	50
51	52	53	54	55	56	57	58	59	60
61	62	63	64	65	66	67	68	69	70
71	72	73	74	75	76	77	78	79	80

Figure 3.17

The error

The child has coloured in 50 squares instead of 50% of the squares.

Why this happens

This may have happened because the child thinks that percentages are always linked to 100 objects. She has not understood that 50% is equivalent to one-half and that we do not always need to have 100 objects. The child may need to return to the 100 square and check for herself what part of the square is coloured for 50%, 25% and so on. Children may not progress effectively with percentages unless they understand the equivalence between percentages and fractions. Children also need to understand the relationship between fractions, decimals and percentages. Lamon (2005, page 217) suggests that shading grids is not a particularly helpful way to teach percentages because children can achieve the answer more quickly in their heads.

Curriculum links		
KS2	Ma2 1a	Make connections in mathematics and appreciate the need to use numerical skills and knowledge when solving problems in other parts of the mathematics curriculum
KS2	Ma2 2f	Understand that 'percentage' means the 'number of parts per 100' and that it can be used for comparisons; find percentages of whole number quantities, using a calculator where appropriate

Ratio and proportion

Given that ratio and proportion are often contextualised in other problems, the issue arises of whether these topics should be taught in context or taught separately. There is no easy solution to this dilemma and teachers may need to try both approaches to support children.

Lamon (2008) explores how the key to understanding fractions, decimals, percentages, ratio and proportion is discussion during reasoning activities. Her book, developed after years of research on this area, develops teacher confidence by asking the same sorts of questions that teachers may ask children. She explains how ratio is a comparison of any two quantities and that it expresses an idea that cannot be expressed by a single number. Additionally, a key premise of the book is about using proportion as a powerful mathematical tool. For example, to know that when two quantities are related to each other and one changes, the other also changes in a precise way, we know that the relationship does not change but that the quantities may increase or decrease. This aids the development of proportional reasoning.

You may find these practical examples helpful.

Ratio: *'for every' – there are three pencils for every child in the class.*
Proportion: *'in every' – there are two red pencils in every pot of pencils.*

3.21 Ratio and proportion

A child is looking at a collection of ribbons. She counts 20 blue ribbons and 10 red ribbons. The teacher asks: *What proportion of the ribbons are red?* She says: *Ten out of twenty.*

The error

The child has confused ratio and proportion.

Why this happens

The difference between ratio and proportion is difficult for children, and sometimes for adults, to understand. The child needs to know that ratio compares **part** with **part** in a set of objects but proportion compares **part** with the **whole** in a set of objects. The proportion of red ribbons is 10 out of 30 or one-third ($\frac{1}{3}$), whereas the ratio of red ribbons to blue ribbons is 10 to 20 or one to two (1:2). The children need to become familiar with the language of ratio and proportion: For ratio they should use *'for every'*. For proportion they should use *'in every'*. Using the language of ratio and proportion regularly will help children to distinguish between these two concepts.

Curriculum links		
KS2	Ma2 1j	Understand and investigate general statements
KS2	Ma2 2g	Recognise approximate proportions of a whole and use simple fractions and percentages to describe them, explaining their methods and reasoning
KS2	Ma2 2h	Solve simple problems involving ratio and direct proportion

Number patterns and sequences

In primary school, children are introduced to number sequences from Reception onwards, though this may not be explicit in curriculum documentation. Counting from 1 to 10 or in 2s forms the basis of understanding number sequences. Number patterns and sequences may be thought of as the building blocks for formal algebra. Nickson (2000, page 117) suggests that the shift of ideas from arithmetic to algebraic is a difficult transition for children and one in which *children tend to carry with them the perspectives and processes established in arithmetic to fall back on.*

3.22 Continuing a simple pattern

The teacher asks the children to complete a pattern (see Figure 3.18).

The error

The child has not continued the pattern that the practitioner began.

Figure 3.18

Why this happens

There are several possible reasons why the child might have done this.

- The child may not have understood the practitioner's question.
- The child may not know that a pattern continues to repeat.
- The child may have wanted to create their own 'pretty' necklace, finding their own design more appealing than the practitioner's.
- The child may have run out of the darker beads, and then later found some.

Curriculum links		
EYFS	Use developing mathematical ideas and methods to solve practical problems	
EYFS	Talk about, recognise and recreate simple patterns	
KS1	Ma2 2b	Create and describe number patterns
KS1	Ma3 1e	Recognise simple spatial patterns and relationships and make predictions about them

3.23 Continuing a number pattern

Having counted on and back in 2s with his class, the teacher decides to introduce counting on in 3s (Figure 3.19). He writes the following number sequence on the whiteboard and then asks what the next number will be. One child responds that the next number will be 18.

The error

The child has counted on two instead of three.

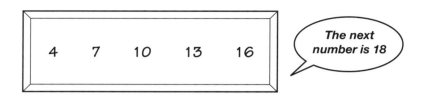

Figure 3.19

Why this happens

There are several possible reasons why the child might have given the wrong answer.

- The child miscounts the numbers. He says to himself: *sixteen, seventeen, eighteen*, instead of counting from 17.
- The child sees the 16 and thinks the numbers are the even numbers he was learning yesterday. If so, then the next even number would be 18.
- The child is still unable to understand symbolic representations of numbers and has been learning counting on in 2s through listening and rote learning. The child therefore gives a *random* response which happens to be 18 but could be any other number.

Curriculum links		
KS1	Ma2 1i	Explain their methods and reasoning when solving problems involving number and data
KS1	Ma2 2b	Create and describe number patterns; explore and record patterns related to addition and subtraction, and then patterns of multiples of 2, 5 and 10 explaining the patterns and using them to make predictions; recognise sequences, including odd and even numbers to 30 then beyond; recognise the relationship between halving and doubling
KS2	Ma2 1k	Search for pattern in their results; develop logical thinking and explain their reasoning
KS2	Ma2 2a	Count on and back in tens or hundreds from any two- or three-digit number; recognise and continue number sequences formed by counting on or back in steps of constant size from any integer, extending to negative integers when counting back
KS2	Ma2 2b	Recognise and describe number patterns, including two- and three-digit multiples of 2, 5 or 10, recognising their patterns and using these to make predictions; make general statements, using words to describe a functional relationship, and test these; recognise prime numbers to 20 and square numbers up to 10 × 10; find factor pairs and all the prime factors of any two-digit integer

Number operations and calculation

Fiona Lawton and Alice Hansen

Chapter overview

This chapter is closely related to Chapter 3. In the Statutory Framework for the Early Years Foundation Stage (DCSF, 2007, page 14) children are expected to be *supported in developing their understanding of problem solving, reasoning and numeracy in a broad range of contexts in which they can explore, enjoy, learn, practise and talk about their developing understanding.* Number operations and calculation can be found in Attainment Target 2 of the National Curriculum for Mathematics in England (DfEE, 1999b). In Key Stage 1 children use informal calculation strategies for the four rules of arithmetic. Throughout Key Stage 2, children are introduced to written calculations with the ultimate aim that they can confidently and accurately use standard methods. Algebraic concepts are embedded within the number Programme of Study for mathematics at both Key Stage 1 and Key Stage 2.

Place value

Since the late 1990s, children have been encouraged to use quantity value (i.e. 43 is 40 plus 3) rather than column value (i.e. 43 is 4 tens and 3 units) in the early stages of learning how to perform calculations. Orton and Frobisher (2005) describe the findings of several research projects which assess children's understanding of place value. The findings are alarming – only 43 per cent of 15-year-old children could identify what the digit '2' represents in the number 521,400 (Orton and Frobisher, 2005, 98). However, children did 'do better' in questions where they were given a number, for example 7 tens, and asked to ring a number containing 7 tens (Orton and Frobisher, 2005, page 98).

Howat (2006) identified that children who were struggling with arithmetic were often unable to use place value effectively. The children had not conceived 'ten' as being able to be ten ones or one ten and this remained the case regardless of her intervention strategies.

To read more about place value in our number system and how children learn place value, read Chapter 3.

4.1 'Borrowing' from zero

A guided group are looking at some vertical subtraction equations with their teacher (see Figure 4.1).

Figure 4.1

The error

The child is using a procedural method of carrying out decomposition, rather than understanding that zero is a place holder in this equation.

Why this happens

Until this lesson, the child has met subtraction algorithms presented in this format that do not require decomposition, and he has learned that to get the answer correct, he needs to 'subtract the digit at the bottom from the digit at the top' each time. He has been shown how to calculate the answer procedurally, rather than building on from earlier methods he was taught. For example, if he had thought about how 70 could be subtracted from 100 and how that might help him to proceed with the calculation, he might have been more successful. Developing more formal algorithms from intuitive mathematics is a more effective way to develop children's use of algorithms like the one in this example (Anghileri, 2000).

Curriculum links

KS2	Ma2 3a	Develop further their understanding of the four number operations and the relationships between them including inverses; use the related vocabulary; choose suitable number operations to solve a given problem, and recognise similar problems to which they apply
KS2	Ma2 3e	Add or subtract any pair of two-digit whole numbers; handle particular cases of three-digit and four-digit additions and subtractions by using compensation or other methods

4.2 Multiplying by 10: 'Adding a zero'

The class is learning the 10 times table. One child says: *Miss, this is easy! You can just add a nought. 3 × 10 is 30, 9 × 10 is 90. So 12 × 10 must be 120.*

The error

The child believes that to multiply by 10, a zero is 'added' to the end of the number.

Why this happens

In mathematics we encourage children to spot patterns and rules. The child has spotted such a pattern. The problem with the child's pattern is that it is not generalisable because the rule only works for whole numbers. While the teacher might praise the child for recognising the pattern, s/he needs to address this misconception to discourage the child from applying this rule to decimal numbers. The child may not understand that when numbers are multiplied by 10 all the digits move one place to the left because they become ten times bigger. The 0 is acting as a place holder in the units/ones column. This can also be seen in other contexts, such as converting between different units of measurement.

Curriculum links		
KS2	Ma2 1j	Understand and investigate general statements
KS2	Ma2 1k	Search for pattern in their results; develop logical thinking and explain their reasoning
KS2	Ma2 2i	Understand and use decimal notation for tenths and hundredths in context (for example, convert a length such as 1.36 metres to centimetres and vice versa); locate on a number line, and order, a set of numbers or measurements; then recognise thousandths (only in metric measurements)
KS2	Ma2 2j	Convert between centimetres and millimetres or metres, then between millimetres and metres, and metres and kilometres, explaining methods and reasoning
KS2	Ma2 3a	Develop further their understanding of the four number operations and the relationships between them including inverses; use the related vocabulary; choose suitable number operations to solve a given problem, and recognise similar problems to which they apply
KS2	Ma2 3h	Multiply and divide, at first in the range 1 to 100 (for example, 27 × 3, 65 ffi 5), then for particular cases of larger numbers by using factors, distribution or other methods

4.3 Multiplication and division by powers of ten: 'moving the decimal point'

Two children have been asked to convert measures in metres to centimetres (see Figure 4.2).

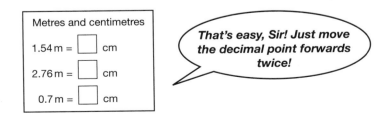

Figure 4.2

The teacher checks their answers and notes that they are all correct. He then asks the children how they calculated their answers. The children tell the teacher that they moved the decimal point 'forwards' twice. They proudly tell the teacher that they remembered to 'add some noughts' onto the 0.7 (i.e. 0.700000) before moving the decimal point.

The error

The children believe that the decimal point moves rather than the digits.

Why this happens

This error may happen because children are constructing their own 'rules' based upon their observations. The children need to understand that the digits move (not the decimal point). The children may not have a clear understanding that the position of a digit determines its value, or that the effect multiplying a number by ten has on making it ten times bigger, so we see each digit move to the left one column.

Curriculum links

KS2	Ma2 1k	Search for pattern in their results; develop logical thinking and explain their reasoning
KS2	Ma2 2c	Read, write and order whole numbers, recognising that the position of a digit gives its value; use correctly the symbols <, >, =; multiply and divide any integer by 10 or 100 then extend to multiplying and dividing by 1000; round integers to the nearest 10 or 100 and then 1000; order a set of negative integers, explaining methods and reasoning; multiply and divide decimals by 10 or 100
KS2	Ma2 3a	Develop further their understanding of the four number operations and the relationships between them including inverses; use the related vocabulary; choose suitable number operations to solve a given problem, and recognise similar problems to which they apply
KS2	Ma2 3f	Recall multiplication facts to 10 × 10 and use them to derive quickly the corresponding division facts
KS2	Ma2 3j	Use written methods for short multiplication and division by a single-digit integer of two-digit then three-digit then four-digit integers, then of numbers with decimals; then use long multiplication, at first for two-digit by two-digit integer calculations, then for three-digit by two-digit calculations; extend division to informal methods of dividing by a two-digit divisor; use approximations and other strategies to check that their answers are reasonable

4.4 Recording the results of calculations

Two children enthusiastically perform several calculations using short multiplication. Here is one of their calculations (Figure 4.3).

$$
\begin{array}{r}
236 \\
\times \quad 8 \\
\hline
1834 \\
\hline
28
\end{array}
$$

Figure 4.3

The error

The children have placed the digits in incorrect columns.

Why this happens

The children have correctly calculated that 8 multiplied by 6 is 48 but have placed the '40' in the units/ones column and the 8 in the tens column. They may not understand that the position of a digit determines its value. The children may need to return to expanded methods of multiplication which use quantity value instead of column value. Alternatively, the error may have happened because the children are trying to use a standard algorithm (written method) which they do not understand. They are possibly attempting to solve the problem by following a set of rules.

Curriculum links		
KS2	Ma2 1i	Communicate mathematically, including the use of precise mathematical language
KS2	Ma2 3j	Use written methods for short multiplication and division by a single-digit integer of two-digit then three-digit then four-digit integers, then of numbers with decimals; then use long multiplication, at first for two-digit by two-digit integer calculations, then for three-digit by two-digit calculations; extend division to informal methods of dividing by a two-digit divisor; use approximations and other strategies to check that their answers are reasonable

4.5 The relative value of money

The teacher introduces a problem-solving activity to his class. He asks the children to find and record as many ways as possible of making 26p. One child draws the solutions shown in Figure 4.4.

Tariq

$$\boxed{20p} + \boxed{6p} = 26p$$

$$\boxed{10p} + \boxed{10p} + \boxed{4p} + \boxed{2p} = 26p$$

Figure 4.4

The error

The child has included coins that do not exist in our currency.

Why this happens

He has used his knowledge of numbers to find solutions to the problem. The child is not aware that some coin values do not exist in our currency. The child may have insufficient experience of handling 'real' money.

Curriculum links		
KS1	Ma2 1a	Approach problems involving number, and data presented in a variety of forms, in order to identify what they need to do
KS1	Ma2 1c	Make decisions about which operations and problem-solving strategies to use
KS1	Ma2 1f	Communicate in spoken, pictorial and written form, at first using informal language and recording, then mathematical language and symbols
KS1	Ma2 1g	Present results in an organised way
KS2	Ma2 1h	Present and interpret solutions in the context of the problem
KS2	Ma2 1k	Search for pattern in their results; develop logical thinking and explain their reasoning
KS2	Ma2 4a	Choose, use and combine any of the four number operations to solve word problems involving numbers in 'real life', money or measures of length, mass, capacity or time, then perimeter and area

Fractions

Fractions are among the most difficult mathematical concepts that children come across at primary school (Charalambous and Pitta-Pantazi, 2005). In fact, analysis of children's errors in fractions has been investigated for many years (see e.g. Brueckner, 1928; Moreton, 1924). Nickson (2000) suggests that children have difficulty applying their knowledge of fractions to problem-solving situations because there are several interpretations of fractions (Chapter 3 describes five) and therefore children do not know which interpretation to use. Lamon (2001, pages 147–148) explains that even students who are studying for a degree in mathematics may have a limited understanding of fractions.

4.6 Fractions as ratios

The teacher asks the class to compare two sets of objects, A and B (Figure 4.5).

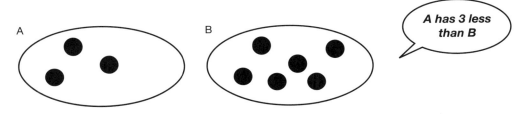

Figure 4.5

One child tells the teacher that set A is 3 less than set B.

The error

The child has used additive comparison instead of multiplicative comparison.

Why this happens

The correct response should be that set A has half as many dots as set B. The child is drawing on her knowledge of addition and subtraction from earlier in her education – when comparing the size of two sets of objects involved using addition/subtraction. She may do this because she does not fully understand the nature of the task. This type of error may also arise when we are comparing lengths. For example, a child may say that object A is 12cm longer than object B instead of saying that object A is 5 times as long as object B.

Curriculum links

KS1	Ma2 1c	Make decisions about which operations and problem-solving strategies to use
KS1	Ma2 2a	Approach problems involving number, and data presented in a variety of forms, in order to identify what they need to do
KS2	Ma2 2d	Understand unit fractions then fractions that are several parts of one whole, locate them on a number line and use them to find fractions of shapes and quantities

4.7 Adding fractions

The child has added $\frac{1}{4} + \frac{1}{2}$ and written the answer as $\frac{2}{6}$ (Figure 4.6).

$$\frac{1}{4} + \frac{1}{2} = \frac{2}{6}$$

Figure 4.6

The error

The child has added the two numerators and then the two denominators to calculate the sum.

Why this happens

The child may have been shown the procedure for multiplying fractions (with the same denominator), and has overgeneralised it to addition. They may not know that to add fractions with different denominators, it is often easier to find equivalent fractions to add together. Whatever the specific reason, it is clear that the child is not aware of what the fractions represent and is carrying out the equation without understanding.

Curriculum links		
KS2	Ma2 2d	Understand unit fractions then fractions that are several parts of one whole, locate them on a number line and use them to find fractions of shapes and quantities
KS2	Ma2 2e	Understand simple equivalent fractions and simplify fractions by cancelling common factors; compare and order simple fractions by converting them to fractions with a common denominator, explaining their methods and reasoning
KS2	Ma2 4c	Estimate answers by approximating and checking that their results are reasonable by thinking about the context of the problem, and where necessary checking accuracy

4.8 Multiplying and dividing by fractions

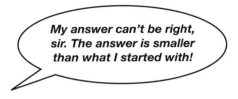

My answer can't be right, sir. The answer is smaller than what I started with!

Figure 4.7

The error

The child has achieved a correct answer, but can't believe it is correct because he holds the belief that the result of a multiplication is always a larger number, and the result of a division is always a smaller number.

Why this happens

The child has created an overgeneralisation from previously working with whole numbers. Earlier work in mathematics about multiplication as repeated addition (where the answer always gets bigger) and division as repeated subtraction (where the answer always reduces) can also compound this misconception (although number-line work with fractions can still be used to explain these answers). Additionally, in everyday language, we talk about animals multiplying (increasing in number), which may cause confusion.

Curriculum links		
KS2	Ma2 2d	Understand unit fractions then fractions that are several parts of one whole, locate them on a number line and use them to find fractions of shapes and quantities
KS2	Ma2 4c	Estimate answers by approximating and checking that their results are reasonable by thinking about the context of the problem, and where necessary checking accuracy

Decimals

According to Sadi (2007), more children have difficulties with decimals than any other number concept. He suggests that this is because of the gap in understanding between the natural numbers and decimal numbers. To read about how decimals are an extension of our whole number system, read Chapter 3.

4.9 Decimal calculations

Two children's answers are shown in Figure 4.8 for a worksheet they were given by their teacher.

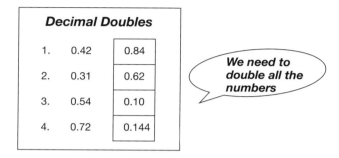

Figure 4.8

The error

The children have doubled all their numbers but failed to take into account that they are decimal numbers.

Why this happens

The children have overgeneralised the rule for doubling which can be applied to whole numbers. They have not taken into account the decimal value of each number. For example, they have calculated that 72 plus 72 is 144 and written 0.144 down. They have not realised what each digit in their answer represents, i.e. 1 unit, 4 tenths and 4 hundredths. This error may be due to a limited understanding of the decimal place-value system.

Similarly, research undertaken by Rees and Barr (cited by Sadi, 2007) found that there were *100 different answers* provided by ten-year-olds for the question 16.36 + 1.9 + 243.075. The most common involved adding the digits before the decimal points and then adding the digits after the decimal point, then combining them to form an answer.

Curriculum links		
KS2	Ma2 1e	Make mental estimates of the answers to calculations; check results
KS2	Ma2 2i	Understand and use decimal notation for tenths and hundredths in context
KS2	Ma2 4c	Estimate answers by approximating and checking that their results are reasonable by thinking about the context of the problem, and where necessary checking accuracy

4.10 Multiplying and dividing decimals

$$60 \times 0.4 = 24$$
$$10 \div 0.1 = 100$$

My calculator is broken. These answers are wrong!

Figure 4.9

The error

The child has found the correct calculation using the calculator, but thinks the answers are wrong.

Why this happens

The child has created an overgeneralisation from previously working with whole numbers. In everyday language, we talk about animals multiplying (increasing in number). Earlier work in mathematics about multiplication as repeated addition (where the answer always gets bigger) and division as repeated subtraction (where the answer always reduces) can also compound this misconception (although number-line work with decimals can still be used to explain these answers).

Curriculum links		
KS2	Ma2 1e	Make mental estimates of the answers to calculations; check results
KS2	Ma2 2i	Understand and use decimal notation for tenths and hundredths in context

Percentages

White *et al.* (2007) discuss how the multiplicative relationship of percentages causes children difficulties. They cite Misailidou and Williams (2003), who showed how 10–14 year olds often used inappropriate additive strategies.

Another difficulty is with the terms 'of' and 'out of' – both of which represent an operator which needs explaining:

'of' – represents the multiplication operator, for example 50% of 80 means 0.5×80;

'out of' – represents the division operator, for example 40 out of 80 means $40 \div 80$.

A key aspect of teaching percentages in the primary school is to help children to understand the relationship between fractions and percentages. Children need to understand that 50%

is equivalent to one-half and 25% is equivalent to one-quarter. This enables children to solve simple percentage problems using a conceptual model based on their understanding of fractions, thus avoiding 'the formula'. If teachers wish to explore more complex problems with some children, they can then use the conceptual model to derive 'the formula' for 'of' problems, so that becomes a natural progression in understanding. Some children will find the concept of percentages very difficult. This may be because their understanding of fractions is weak. In these cases, teachers will need to return to earlier concepts relating to fractions, including concrete representations of part of a set and part of a whole.

To read about children developing the notion of percent, read Chapter 3.

4.11 Percentages as a proportion

The class is calculating percentage discounts. One question requires the children to calculate the cost of two bikes, both having a 10% discount applied. One pair decides to find the total of the full cost of the bikes, and then deduct 20% from the total.

The error

The pair has decided to deduct 20% from the total, instead of 10%.

Why this happens

The children are combining the percentages as absolute amounts (and use inappropriate additive strategies), rather than as a proportion of the price.

Curriculum links		
KS2	Ma2 2f	Understand that 'percentage' means the 'number of parts per 100' and that it can be used for comparisons; find percentages of whole-number quantities, using a calculator where appropriate

Ratio and proportion

Much research in the area of proportional reasoning identifies that solving ratio and proportion problems is a very difficult task for most children and student teachers (Misailidou and Williams, 2002). Similarly to the research discussed above on percentages, Ryan and Williams (2007) also identify multiplicative versus additive strategies as a barrier to solving ratio and proportion problems. They explain how, on occasion, additive strategies can work (for example in the case of 1:2 or 1:n, it is possible to count on in order to solve the problems) but that most problems in any ratio m:n cannot work by using additive strategies. Their research identifies how many children prefer to add or subtract numbers in problems, and avoid multiplication, division and particularly fractions.

You can read more about ratio and proportion and its relationship with fractions in Chapter 3.

4.12 The multiplicative nature of direct proportion

A group of children want to bake a cake for four people. They have found a recipe for two people, so they need to calculate the ingredients they will require to bake a cake for four people. The recipe and the children's amendments are shown in Figure 4.10.

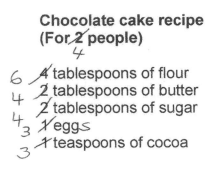

Chocolate cake recipe
(For 2 people)
4

6   4 tablespoons of flour
4   2 tablespoons of butter
    2 tablespoons of sugar
4   3 eggs
3   1 teaspoons of cocoa
3

Figure 4.10

The error

The children have added two more of each ingredient to the recipe for two people.

Why this happens

The children do not understand the multiplicative nature of direct proportion. (See also 'Fractions as ratios'.) The children have used an additive rule instead of a multiplicative rule. They have done this because they think that if we have two more people then we need two more of each ingredient. This is a common difficulty with direct proportion.

Curriculum links		
KS2	Ma2 1a	Make connections in mathematics and appreciate the need to use numerical skills and knowledge when solving problems in other parts of the mathematics curriculum
KS2	Ma2 1h	Present and interpret solutions in the context of the problem
KS2	Ma2 2h	Solve simple problems involving ratio and direct proportion
KS2	Ma2 4b	Choose and use an appropriate way to calculate and explain their methods and reasoning

The four rules of arithmetic (addition, subtraction, multiplication, division)

Counting forms the building blocks of arithmetic. Imagine a set of three objects and a set of four objects and a child wants to find the total number of objects. (To read further about counting, see Chapter 3.) There are five ways they could identify the total. They could:

Count-all: *one, two, three, four, five, six, seven;*

Count-on: The child counts on from the first set: *four, five, six, seven;*

Count-on from the larger: *five, six, seven;*

Count-on from either: *four, five six, seven* **or** *five, six, seven* (and know that the answer will be the same);

Known facts: The child just knows three plus four equals seven.

What appears to be clear from research (e.g. Carpenter and Moser, 1979; Steffe *et al.*, 1982; Foster, 1994; Gray and Tall, 1994) is that less able children are more likely to rely on concrete counting methods whereas more able children have a more flexible and abstract approach. Orton and Frobisher (2005, page 13) suggest that this may be to do with memory: *the more readily one remembers the easier it is to think … [and so] less effort is required in pulling essential information to the forefront of the mind* (see Chapter 1 for discussion about working memory and long-term memory to explain this further). Boaler (2009) suggests that children who are involved in talking about different mental calculation strategies are able to see how thinking flexibly about number can help approach problems in different ways.

Hall (2000) explains to us the importance of Piaget's argument that thought is internalised action. According to Piaget, children do not have the ability to start to use *mental actions* until they are about seven years old. If this is the case, then it is not surprising that children have difficulty understanding the concept of abstract numerals. However, research undertaken by Carruthers and Worthington published in a book described as *the most important book on emergent mathematical thought ever written* (Matthews, in Carruthers and Worthington, 2006) identify how children's mark making is the way that they make their own meanings of mathematical ideas, often devising their own representations from a very young age.

4.13 'Take away' and 'difference'

A guided group have been asked what is the difference between 6 and 9. One child responds with, *Well, they look the same if you stand on your head.*

The error

The child has used the everyday meaning for 'difference', identifying that '6' and '9' are essentially the same figure rotated. She has not considered the mathematical difference of these.

Why this happens

The child may have experienced more questions involving 'take away' (*what is nine take away six?*). The term 'difference' may be new and she has fallen back onto the more familiar interpretation she has. Using models to demonstrate how the processes for taking away or finding the difference are quite different may be one way to help understanding.

Curriculum links		
EYFS		Begin to relate subtraction to 'taking away'
EYFS		Use language such as 'more' or 'less' to compare two numbers
KS1	Ma2 1f	Communicate in spoken, pictorial and written form, at first using informal language and recording, then mathematical language and symbols
KS1	Ma2 3a	Understand addition and use related vocabulary; recognise that addition can be done in any order; understand subtraction as both 'take away' and 'difference' and use the related vocabulary
KS2	Ma2 1h	Present and interpret solutions in the context of the problem
KS2	Ma2 1i	Communicate mathematically, including the use of precise mathematical language
KS2	Ma2 3a	Develop further their understanding of the four number operations and the relationships between them including inverses; use the related vocabulary; choose suitable number operations to solve a given problem, and recognise similar problems to which they apply

4.14 'Sum'

A teacher overhears two children discussing their answers. One child asks, *'what have you got for that division sum?'*

The error

The child has used 'sum' in an incorrect context. 'Sum' should only be used for addition, and no other operations.

Why this happens

Colloquially, people refer to 'maths sums'. However, to be mathematically correct, a sum is the result of adding two or more numbers (addend + addend = sum), the *summation* of the numbers. In this case, the child could been have asked, *Have you found the quotient?* (dividend ÷ divisor = quotient).

Curriculum links		
EYFS		In practical activities and discussion, begin to use the vocabulary involved in adding and subtracting
KS1	Ma2 1e	Use the correct language, symbols and vocabulary associated with number and data
KS1	Ma2 1f	Communicate in spoken, pictorial and written form, at first using informal language and recording, then mathematical language and symbols
KS1	Ma2 3a	Understand addition and use related vocabulary
KS2	Ma2 1i	Communicate mathematically, including the use of precise mathematical language
KS2	Ma2 3a	Develop further their understanding of the four number operations and the relationships between them including inverses; use the related vocabulary; choose suitable number operations to solve a given problem, and recognise similar problems to which they apply
KS2	Ma2 4b	Choose and use an appropriate way to calculate and explain their methods and reasoning

4.15 Addition and subtraction of single-digit numbers

Two children have been asked to complete number sentences. Two of their answers are given in Figure 4.11.

Figure 4.11

The error

This is a counting error.

Why this happens

The children have counted the starting number twice in each calculation. For 3 + 4, they have counted: *three, four, five, six*. For 7 – 5, they have counted *seven, six, five, four, three*. Many young children make this error. Encouraging young children to play board games where they count on from the next square may help them to calculate number sentences accurately.

Curriculum links		
KS1	Ma2 1e	Use the correct language, symbols and vocabulary associated with number and data
KS1	Ma2 2a	Approach problems involving number, and data presented in a variety of forms, in order to identify what they need to do
KS1	Ma2 3a	Understand addition and use related vocabulary; recognise that addition can be done in any order; understand subtraction as both 'take away' and 'difference' and use the related vocabulary; recognise that subtraction is the inverse of addition; give the subtraction corresponding to an addition and vice versa; use the symbol '=' to represent equality; solve simple missing number problems (for example, 6 = 2 + ?)

4.16 Mathematical symbols

A teacher asks a guided group to complete some number sentences. Figure 4.12 shows the questions and one child's responses.

Figure 4.12

The error

The child has confused the × symbol with the + symbol and the ÷ with the − symbol.

Why this happens

Mathematical symbols are abstract representations. In this case they represent mathematical operations. The multiplication and addition symbols are visually similar, as are the division and subtraction symbols. Children may find it difficult to distinguish between each pair of symbols. It may also be that the child has a poor conceptual understanding of multiplication and division so reverts to the more familiar concepts of addition and subtraction. Children need to have a sound understanding of the underlying concepts alongside the introduction of symbols.

Curriculum links		
KS1	Ma2 1e	Use the correct language, symbols and vocabulary associated with number and data
KS1	Ma2 3a	Understand addition and use related vocabulary; recognise that addition can be done in any order; understand subtraction as both 'take away' and 'difference' and use the related vocabulary; recognise that subtraction is the inverse of addition; give the subtraction corresponding to an addition and vice versa; use the symbol '=' to represent equality; solve simple missing-number problems (for example, 6 = 2 + ?)
KS2	Ma2 3a	Develop further their understanding of the four number operations and the relationships between them including inverses; use the related vocabulary; choose suitable number operations to solve a given problem, and recognise similar problems to which they apply
KS2	Ma2 1g	Use notation diagrams and symbols correctly within a given problem

4.17 Finding an unknown in a number sentence

A child has been asked to complete the number sentence shown in Figure 4.13.

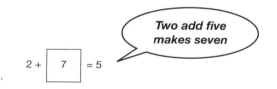

$$2 + \boxed{7} = 5$$

Two add five makes seven

Figure 4.13

He writes '7' in the empty box.

The error

The child has added 2 to 5 to obtain 7.

Why this happens

The child may be familiar with number sentences of the type $2 + 3 = \Box$, so he sees the addition sign and adds the two numbers together. The child may not realise that the question is asking, *How many more are needed to make five?*

Alternatively, a subtraction calculation could be used. It may be that he does not understand that subtraction is the inverse of addition. Using subtraction is difficult for children because it requires children to solve an algebraic equation of the type $32 + x = 57$, and should not be used until they have a good understanding of counting on to find the answer.

Curriculum links

KS1	Ma2 1e	Use the correct language, symbols and vocabulary associated with number and data
KS1	Ma2 3a	Understand addition and use related vocabulary; recognise that addition can be done in any order; understand subtraction as both 'take away' and 'difference' and use the related vocabulary; recognise that subtraction is the inverse of addition; give the subtraction corresponding to an addition and vice versa; use the symbol '=' to represent equality; solve simple missing number problems (for example, $6 = 2 + ?$)
KS1	Ma2 4a	Choose sensible calculation methods to solve whole-number problems (including problems involving money or measures), drawing on their understanding of the operations
KS2	Ma2 1g	Use notation diagrams and symbols correctly within a given problem
KS2	Ma2 3a	Develop further their understanding of the four number operations and the relationships between them including inverses; use the related vocabulary; choose suitable number operations to solve a given problem, and recognise similar problems to which they apply

4.18 Place-value errors

The following examples illustrate place-value errors.

Example 1: addition and subtraction

Figure 4.14

The errors

(a) Failure to understand that the position of a digit determines its value. The 5 has been placed in the tens column instead of the units column.

(b) Failure to understand that the position of a digit determines its value. An additional column has been added. The child is unaware that 14 equals 1 ten and 4 units.

(c) Failure to understand that the position of a digit determines its value. The child has reversed the tens and units digits when carrying.

(d) Failure to understand that the hundreds column exists even when no digits reside in it initially.

(e) Failure to understand the value of the digits in the answer. The child has reversed the tens and hundreds digits when writing the answer.

(f) Lack of understanding about decomposition. The child does not understand the principle of exchange, for example exchanging 1 ten for 10 ones.

Example 2: multiplication and division

(a)
$$\begin{array}{r} 24 \\ \times\,3 \\ \hline 612 \\ 1 \end{array}$$

(b)
$$\begin{array}{r} 36 \\ \times\,3 \\ \hline 08 \\ 1 \end{array}$$

(c)
$$\begin{array}{r} 47 \\ \times\,23 \\ \hline 141 \\ 94 \\ \hline 235 \end{array}$$

(d)
$$\begin{array}{r} 33 \\ 3\overline{)909} \end{array}$$

Figure 4.15

The errors

(a) Failure to understand the position of a digit determines its value. The carrying digit has been inserted in the answer in the tens column. The answer to 3×20 has been placed in the hundreds column instead of the tens column.

(b) Failure to understand the position of a digit determines its value. The child has not created a hundreds column.

(c) Failure to understand the position of a digit determines its value. The child has treated the tens digit multiplication as if it were a units digit multiplication. The child does not understand that the '2' in 23 is actually two tens or 20.

(d) Lack of understanding of the role of zero as a place holder. The child doesn't realise that 0 must be used to preserve the place value in the answer.

Why this happens

The number operations errors above usually occur because the child has been introduced to standard written methods which s/he does not understand because s/he does not have a clear understanding of place value. Often children are trying to perform the calculations procedurally, by following poorly understood rules. Answers will remain incorrect or unchecked if children do not use approximation to check their answers.

Curriculum links

KS1	Ma2 1e	Use the correct language, symbols and vocabulary associated with number and data
KS1	Ma2 3a	Understand addition and use related vocabulary; recognise that addition can be done in any order; understand subtraction as both 'take away' and 'difference' and use the related vocabulary; recognise that subtraction is the inverse of addition; give the subtraction corresponding to an addition and vice versa; use the symbol '=' to represent equality; solve simple missing number problems (for example, 6 = 2 + ?)
KS2	Ma2 1e	Make mental estimates of the answers to calculations; check results
KS2	Ma2 2c	Read, write and order whole numbers, recognising that the position of a digit gives its value; use correctly the symbols <, >, =; multiply and divide any integer by 10 or 100 then extend to multiplying and dividing by 1000; round integers to the nearest 10 or 100 and then 1000; order a set of negative integers, explaining methods and reasoning; multiply and divide decimals by 10 or 100
KS2	Ma2 3a	Develop further their understanding of the four number operations and the relationships between them including inverses; use the related vocabulary; choose suitable number operations to solve a given problem, and recognise similar problems to which they apply
KS2	Ma2 3i	Use written methods to add and subtract positive integers less than 1000, then up to 10000, then add and subtract numbers involving decimals; use approximations and other strategies to check that their answers are reasonable
KS2	Ma2 3j	Use written methods for short multiplication and division by a single-digit integer of two-digit then three-digit then four-digit integers, then of numbers with decimals; then use long multiplication, at first for two-digit by two-digit integer calculations, then for three-digit by two-digit calculations; extend division to informal methods of dividing by a two-digit divisor; use approximations and other strategies to check that their answers are reasonable
KS2	Ma2 4b	Choose and use an appropriate way to calculate and explain their methods and reasoning

4.19 Overgeneralisation errors

The following examples illustrate overgeneralisation errors.

Example 1: addition and subtraction

(a)
$$
\begin{array}{r}
374 \\
-\ 158 \\
\hline
224
\end{array}
$$

(b)
$$
\begin{array}{r}
4\cancel{5}^{1}9 \\
-\ 28 \\
\hline
211
\end{array}
$$

Figure 4.16

The errors

(a) The child has overgeneralised the commutative law, which applies to addition but not to subtraction.
(b) Overgeneralisation of the need for decomposition.

Why this happens

In example (a) the child has actually found the difference between 4 and 8. When learning number bonds, children are encouraged to find the difference between numbers. Often in our questioning of children we ask, *What is the difference between 8 and 4?* or, *What is the difference between 4 and 8?* We make no distinction between the two questions so children use this logic when performing standard calculations. In example (b) the child is likely to be following 'rules'. S/he may have been introduced to decomposition and is now applying this 'new rule' to all calculations. The child may also have a weak understanding of place value. Answers will remain incorrect if children are not using approximation to check their answers.

Example 2: multiplication and division

(a)
$$
\begin{array}{r}
423 \\
3\overline{)1279}
\end{array}
$$

(b)
$$
\begin{array}{r}
34 \\
\times\ 23 \\
\hline
1020 \\
680 \\
\hline
1700
\end{array}
$$

(c)
$$
\begin{array}{r|l}
\text{hrs} & \text{mins} \\
3 & 35 \\
\times\ 5 & \\
\hline
16 & 75 = 16\frac{3}{4}\ \text{hours}
\end{array}
$$

Figure 4.17

The errors

(a) The child has overgeneralised the 'rule' for short multiplication. S/he has divided the units/ones digits first then the tens and finally the hundreds. The child has worked right to left instead of left to right.

(b) The child has overgeneralised the rule 'put down a zero' for multiplication by the tens digit. The child has placed a zero in the units multiplied by units row.

(c) The child has overgeneralised base-ten methods of calculation. S/he has used base ten methods for the multiplication of minutes. The child has seen the calculation as a 'decimal' calculation.

Why this happens

In all of the cases above the child has learned a 'rule' and then applied it inappropriately. This probably occurs because the child has a poor understanding of the methods to which s/he has been introduced. Answers will remain incorrect if children are not using approximation to check their answers.

Curriculum links

KS2	Ma2 1e	Make mental estimates of the answers to calculations; check results
KS2	Ma2 3a	Develop further their understanding of the four number operations and the relationships between them including inverses; use the related vocabulary; choose suitable number operations to solve a given problem, and recognise similar problems to which they apply
KS2	Ma2 3i	Use written methods to add and subtract positive integers less than 1000, then up to 10,000, then add and subtract numbers involving decimals; use approximations and other strategies to check that their answers are reasonable
KS2	Ma2 3j	Use written methods for short multiplication and division by a single-digit integer of two-digit then three-digit then four-digit integers, then of numbers with decimals; then use long multiplication, at first for two-digit by two-digit integer calculations, then for three-digit by two-digit calculations; extend division to informal methods of dividing by a two-digit divisor; use approximations and other strategies to check that their answers are reasonable
KS2	Ma2 4b	Choose and use an appropriate way to calculate and explain their methods and reasoning
KS2	Ma2 4c	Estimate answers by approximating and checking that their results are reasonable by thinking about the context of the problem, and where necessary checking accuracy

4.20 Undergeneralisation errors

A teacher is introducing her children to mentally calculating the sum of two two-digit numbers. She wants the children to partition the multiples of 10. She shows the children the following examples on the whiteboard (Figure 4.18, A). She asks them to practise this idea. Figure 4.18, B shows one child's response to two of the calculations.

14 + 15 = 10 + 10 + 4 + 5
So, 14 + 15 = 29

12 + 13 = 10 + 10 + 2 + 3
So, 12 + 13 = 25

4.18, A

1.   24 + 42 = 10 + 10 + 4 + 2
So, 24 + 42 = 26

2.   18 + 19 = 10 + 10 + 8 + 9
So, 18 + 19 = 2107

4.18, B

Figure 4.18

The errors

1 The child has copied the teacher's method and partitioned the numbers into one lot of 10 then the units.

2 The child writes down the '2' from the 10 + 10 then works out that 8 + 9 is 17. He partitions the 17 into 10 + 7 and then writes both numbers down next to his '2'.

Why this happens

These errors occur because the child has not encountered sufficient examples of the methods being taught. The child is unable to abstract the underpinning concepts which make the method 'work'. The child then tries to develop his own method to solve the problem.

Curriculum links		
KS2	Ma2 1e	Make mental estimates of the answers to calculations; check results
KS2	Ma2 3i	Use written methods to add and subtract positive integers less than 1000, then up to 10,000, then add and subtract numbers involving decimals; use approximations and other strategies to check that their answers are reasonable
KS2	Ma2 3j	Use written methods for short multiplication and division by a single-digit integer of two-digit then three-digit then four-digit integers, then of numbers with decimals; then use long multiplication, at first for two-digit by two-digit integer calculations, then for three-digit by two-digit calculations; extend division to informal methods of dividing by a two-digit divisor; use approximations and other strategies to check that their answers are reasonable

KS2	Ma2 4b	Choose and use an appropriate way to calculate and explain their methods and reasoning
KS2	Ma2 4c	Estimate answers by approximating and checking that their results are reasonable by thinking about the context of the problem, and where necessary checking accuracy

Solving numerical word problems

Word problems have been in education for many centuries – it is possible to find verbal problems almost 4000 years ago in Ancient Egyptian artefacts, as well as in other ancient manuscripts from China and India (Verschaffel *et al.*, 2000). Verschaffel *et al.* (2000) suggest that it is possible to infer why word problems have been used in mathematics education. They can:

- offer practice of mathematical skills in an everyday context;
- motivate children, by convincing them mathematics is useful and necessary;
- assess children's attainment;
- develop children's creative/problem-solving abilities;
- develop new mathematical concepts and skills.

Newman's (1977) five-step framework is commonly used by researchers to consider how numerical word problems are solved. In order to successfully answer a word problem, a child must:

- **read** (or decode) the question;
- **comprehend** the symbols, and the area of mathematics used in the question;
- **transform** that comprehension to be able to select an appropriate process to solve the problem;
- use **process skills** to carry out the process identified above;
- **encode** the answer within the original question to provide an appropriate answer.

At the same time, the child must avoid any careless errors. If following this framework, teachers need to be aware of the difficulties children may have at the first three stages and try to match the words and/or symbols and comprehension level to the children's attainment levels. Often we focus on solving number problems which have already been *transformed* into calculations for children so they do not have the opportunity to learn or practise how to read, comprehend and transform word problems.

There continues great debate as to the place and value of word problems in school, including argument that they are artificial and unrelated to the real world. Recent and ongoing work on mathematics education in Holland, reported in Anghileri (2001), suggests that children should be introduced to problems that are meaningful to them as part of their mathematical learning. Advocates of Realistic Mathematics Education (RME) (Anghileri, 2001) argue that *if children learn mathematics in an isolated fashion, divorced from experienced reality, it will be quickly forgotten and the children will not be able to apply it* (page 51). Dutch educators have developed key goals of primary school mathematics using the RME approach, one of which is to *apply standard algorithms in ... easy context situations* (page 58).

4.21 Word problems

Four word problems follow to exemplify the complexity of solving numerical word problems.

Example 1

The children have been presented with the following problem.

On Joel's birthday he was given a model car worth £9.00. The next week, Joanne received a doll worth £7.00. How much more was spent on Joel?

A child says sixteen.

The error

The child has added seven and nine together instead of subtracting £7.00 from £9.00. Instead of counting on or using subtraction, she has chosen an operator she is comfortable using: addition. She has also not encoded the answer so that it fits in with the original context of money.

Why this happens:

There are several reasons why the child might have been unable to solve this problem correctly.

- There is superfluous information in the problem, for example 'Joel's birthday' and 'The next week'. This causes 'interference' in the child's ability to *transform* the problem into a calculation.
- The names Joel and Joanne are quite similar visually so this may confuse the reader.
- This is a comparison problem, which is more difficult than a 'take away' problem.
- The problem contains gender stereotyping. The child might wonder why Joel gets a car and Joanne a doll. This problem may not match her everyday experiences.

Example 2

A child was asked to solve the following word problem.

Helen had some money. She gave away 12p to her brother and now has 37 pence left. How much money did Helen have to start with?

She says that Helen has 25 pence.

The error

The child has subtracted 12p from 37p. She has selected the wrong operation.

Why this happens

There are several reasons why the child might have been unable to solve this problem correctly.

- The words 'gave away' may imply subtraction. The child may have focused on these words to select the operation.
- The order of the numbers in the problem does not correspond to the chronological order of events.
- This is a complementary subtraction problem which is more difficult than a combination problem.

Example 3

Two children have been asked to solve the following problem.

Stephen already has £42 in his bank savings account. He wants to buy a dog. How much money will he have if he earns 75p every day for 6 weeks?

They say he will have £492.

The errors

The children have calculated that 75×6 is 450 and then assumed this is £450, which they have added to the £42 pounds that Stephen already has. The children have made two errors. Firstly they have not calculated that there are 42 days in 6 weeks so they have just multiplied 75 by 6. Secondly, they have not changed the answer in pence into pounds before adding it to the original amount.

Why this happens

There are several reasons why the children may have been unable to solve this problem correctly.

- The problem is a two-step problem which is more complex. It contains a mix of operations: multiplication and addition.
- There is a mix of units (£ and pence). This means that the children have to either multiply decimal numbers (0.75) or remember to represent their answer in pounds not pence.
- There is superfluous information in the question, for example, 'He wants to buy a dog'.
- The children may not recognise (or may forget) that the phrase 'every day' implies multiplying by 7 (the number of days in a week) because the number 7 cannot be seen in the problem.
- The children may have assumed their answer is correct when they compare their answer with their everyday knowledge of the price of buying a dog.

Curriculum links		
For all examples, the curriculum links are:		
KS1	Ma2 1c	Make decisions about which operations and problem-solving strategies to use
KS1	Ma2 4a	Choose sensible calculation methods to solve whole-number problems (including problems involving money or measures), drawing on their understanding of the operations
KS1	Ma2 4b	Choose and use an appropriate way to calculate and explain their methods and reasoning
KS2	Ma2 1b	Break down a more complex problem or calculation into simpler steps before attempting a solution; identify the information needed to carry out the tasks
KS2	Ma2 1e	Make mental estimates of the answers to calculations; check results
KS2	Ma2 4a	Choose, use and combine any of the four number operations to solve word problems involving numbers in 'real life', money or measures of length, mass, capacity or time, then perimeter and area
KS2	Ma2 4b	Choose and use an appropriate way to calculate and explain their methods and reasoning
KS2	Ma2 4c	Estimate answers by approximating and checking that their results are reasonable by thinking about the context of the problem, and where necessary checking accuracy

Number relationships (pre-algebra)

Algebra is often difficult to learn, as children need to master the language to be able to use it. However, Warren (2004) suggests a reason why 12–13 year old children may find it difficult to find the functional relationship between growing patterns and their position, and use this generalisation to generate other visual patterns for other positions. She suggests that prior pattern development in primary schools is simply related to growing patterns. Her research suggests that *young children are not only capable of thinking about the relationship between two data sets but also of expressing this relationship in a very abstract form* (Page 311).

Koedinger and Nathan (2004) identified how children were more successful solving simple algebra story problems than solving mathematically equivalent equations. They explained the reason for this was that children had difficulties comprehending the formal symbolic representations but were able to use the situated knowledge to facilitate their problem-solving performance.

Ainley *et al.* (2009, page 417) suggest further activities that primary-aged children can undertake to prepare them for formal algebra at secondary school. These are:

- *structuring and generalising*: analysing, describing and continuing patterns and structures in geometric and algebraic contexts;
- *representing*: using actions, gestures, signs and artefacts to bridge the gap to using alphanumeric symbols.

Ainley *et al.* (2005) report that spreadsheets are an effective tool to support children's algebraic development. They explain how the careful design of tasks that are purposeful for children, and contain opportunity to appreciate the utility of algebra, can support the transition of children from Key Stage 2 to Key Stage 3.

4.22 Algebraic variables

A guided mathematics group is converting pounds to Euros with the teacher. They complete together Table 4.1, but when they approach the final column, one child states, *That's impossible sir, you can't have n pounds!*

Pounds	1	2	3	4	5	10	50	n
Euros	1.22	2.44	3.66	4.88	6.10	12.20	61.00	

Table 4.1 Conversion task

The error

The child does not understand what 'n' represents in the question.

Why this happens

The child does not understand the concept of a variable. She does not understand that 'n' can be used to represent any number of pounds. The child is falling back on arithmetic ideas to answer the question. She can understand the question when she can relate it to 'real' money but she is unable to abstract the relationship between the two currencies. The concept that the teacher is asking her to understand may be too complex for her and perhaps introduced in a way which is beyond her experience.

Curriculum links

KS2	Ma2 2b	Recognise and describe number patterns, including two- and three-digit multiples of 2, 5 or 10, recognising their patterns and using these to make predictions; make general statements, using words to describe a functional relationship, and test these
KS2	Ma2 2h	Solve simple problems involving ratio and direct proportion
KS2	Ma2 4d	Recognise, represent and interpret simple number relationships, constructing and using formulae in words then symbols

5

Shape and space

Alice Hansen

Chapter overview

The first aspect of mathematics that young children explore is shape and space. As soon as they begin to interact with the three-dimensional world they live in, babies begin to learn about their position in space and how this is related to other objects. In time children learn to become aware of a two-dimensional representation of their world and this continues to develop into spatial reasoning.

The Statutory Framework for the Early Years Foundation Stage (DCSF, 2007) is mainly concerned with children naming shapes and recreating patterns with shapes. Shape and space, along with measures, form Attainment Target 3 of the National Curriculum for England. It is interested in using and applying shape and space, understanding properties of shape and understanding properties of position and movement. Key Stage 1 children should be developing their language of shape and space while Key Stage 2 children will be involved with two- and three-dimensional shapes and their properties, position and direction, and transformation. This chapter will consider aspects of three-dimensional and two-dimensional shape and space, angle and position and movement to include the aspects of symmetry (including reflection), rotation, translation and enlargement.

Three- and two-dimensional shapes

Although the topic of shape and space is the first aspect of mathematics that children begin to interact with, it is a complex subject. Teachers need to be aware of its complexity in order to help them to identify the difficulties that are likely to arise for children. From a young age, children begin to draw, making sense of the three-dimensional world around them by representing it in two dimensions (Ring, 2001). This is a form of language (visual) that should be considered as important as other types of more conventional languages such as written or spoken (Hall, 2007).

It is the representation of shapes in our environment that can make early understanding of properties and definitions of 3D and 2D shape difficult. This is because children are continually surrounded by prototypical shapes (Walcott *et al.*, 2009). These have an overwhelming impact on the visual images that they develop. Much research illustrates that children tend to limit their understanding of shapes to the examples they are shown (see, for example, Yin, 2003). Even when children learn the definition of a 2D or 3D shape, the prototypical visual image they have often remains (Hershkowitz *et al.*, 1990). It is our responsibility as teachers to ensure that children are exposed to shapes of varying size, orientation and type, to broaden their limited understanding of shape.

Another aspect that compounds the nature of shape and space is the inclusivity and exclusivity of definitions. Children find it difficult to consider that a square is a rectangle (demonstrating the inclusive nature of the definition of rectangles), particularly when they are faced with images in and out of school where what they call a rectangle is a prototypical oblong (illustrating the exclusive nature of the definition of oblong: a rectangle that is not a square (see, for example, Hansen, 2008; Jones, 2000; Monaghan, 2000). Orton (2005, page 150) highlights that *there can be confusion when one is talking to children about squares and rectangles, because children tend to classify these shapes as different, whereas mathematicians prefer to think of squares as special rectangles. To avoid this difficulty, some books use the word oblong for a non-square rectangle.*

Finally, the large variety of ways that shapes can be defined also adds to the issues of complexity. For example, we can consider the length of the individual, parallel or adjacent sides, the size of the interior angles, the order of rotation and the lines of symmetry. Lehrer *et al.* (1998) found, worryingly, that over time, children were less likely to notice attributes (such as sides or vertices) because of the conventional way geometry is being taught.

Geometry's roots lie in young children being able to manipulate objects. Physical manipulation of objects in geometry teaching has been used for over a century (e.g. Hill, 1908), and more recently the affordances that manipulation within virtual learning environments give learners have been greatly documented also (Bouck and Flanagan, 2009; Hansen, 2008). Manipulation supports visualisation, a vital skill that children need in order to develop their geometrical understanding (Mulligan *et al.*, 2004). It also helps children to build essential mental representations (Kelly, 2006).

Resources also offer a platform for children's discussion. High-quality talk in all areas of mathematics is essential (DfES, 2008; DfE, 2010). However, there are, in fact, few findings related to young children talking about shape (Garrick, 2002). Coltman *et al.* (2002) identified the role of a supporting adult in supporting young children's understanding of aspects of 3D shape. Scaffolding and talk through structured adult intervention were shown to increase the effectiveness of learning, which in turn lead to children's secure and transferable knowledge. In an earlier, related study, Anghileri and Baron (1999) found that when sorting, children did not undertake any discussion that may have led to clarifying tasks. This was also found in Saads and Davis's (1997) study on the importance of language in the development of children's geometrical understanding. They state, *discussion involving the names and characteristics of the 3D shapes is necessary for children to clarify mathematical understanding, for example in the relationships between cubes and squares* (page 17). Likewise, Hasegawa (1997) identified that if a child does not understand concepts such as edges, sides, corners and faces, the definitions of shapes are meaningless.

5.1 Construction using three-dimensional objects

The child finds it difficult to build a stable tower and it continually topples over.

The error

The child is placing unstable blocks at the bottom of the tower.

Why this happens

From an early age, children begin to manipulate three-dimensional objects, including building tall constructions. They need to learn which shapes are the best for various parts of the tower. This is essential for children to develop their spatial understanding and reasoning. Children who continue to build unstable constructions may have been limited in the shapes or materials they have used.

Curriculum links		
EYFS		Use developing mathematical ideas and methods to solve practical problems
EYFS		Use everyday words to describe position
EYFS		Use language such as 'circle' to describe the shape and size of solids and flat shapes
KS1	Ma3 1a	Try different approaches and find ways of overcoming difficulties when solving shape and space problems
KS1	Ma3 1c	Select and use appropriate equipment and materials when solving shape and space problems
KS1	Ma3 2a	Describe properties of shapes that they can see or visualise using the related vocabulary
KS1	Ma3 2b	Observe, handle and describe common 2D and 3D shapes; name and describe the mathematical features of common 2D and 3D shapes, including triangles of various kinds, rectangles including squares, circles, cubes, cuboids, then hexagons, pentagons, cylinders, pyramids, cones and spheres
KS1	Ma3 2c	Create 2D shapes and 3D shapes

5.2 Mathematical terminology in three-dimensional shape and space: faces

Figure 5.1 The child finds it difficult to use the term the 'face' on a 3D shape.

Why this happens

From an early age, children have conversations at home and in school about the *sides* of an object. When they are introduced to the term *face*, it can be confusing and difficult as they may have been used to using this term in different ways, some non-mathematically. Without understanding the meaning of the term *face*, it is meaningless for children to begin to define three-dimensional objects.

Curriculum links		
KS1	Ma3 2a	Describe properties of shapes that they can see or visualise using the related vocabulary
KS1	Ma3 2b	Observe, handle and describe common 2D and 3D shapes; name and describe the mathematical features of common 2D and 3D shapes, including triangles of various kinds, rectangles including squares, circles, cubes, cuboids, then hexagons, pentagons, cylinders, pyramids, cones and spheres
KS2	Ma3 2b	Visualise and describe 2D and 3D shapes and the way they behave, making more precise use of geometrical language, especially that of triangles, quadrilaterals, and prisms and pyramids of various kinds

5.3 Mathematical terminology in three-dimensional shape and space: vertices

Figure 5.2

The error

The child finds it difficult to identify the vertex of a 3D shape and wants to call it a corner.

Why this happens

Children have conversations at home and in Key Stage 1 at school about the *corners* of an object. When they are introduced to the terms *vertex* and *vertices*, it can be confusing and difficult because they may not have used these terms before.

Curriculum links		
KS1	Ma3 2a	Describe properties of shapes that they can see or visualise using the related vocabulary
KS1	Ma3 2b	Observe, handle and describe common 2D and 3D shapes; name and describe the mathematical features of common 2D and 3D shapes, including triangles of various kinds, rectangles including squares, circles, cubes, cuboids, then hexagons, pentagons, cylinders, pyramids, cones and spheres
KS2	Ma3 2b	Visualise and describe 2D and 3D shapes and the way they behave, making more precise use of geometrical language, especially that of triangles, quadrilaterals, and prisms and pyramids of various kinds

5.4 Nets

Figure 5.3

The error

The child finds it difficult to visualise which nets will form a cube.

Why this happens

Children who haven't had a lot of experience in visualising 3D shapes being opened up and folded again, often find it difficult to imagine the net of a shape or 'see' a net being folded to make a 3D shape. They may have learnt that the common cross shape (Figure 5.3, left) is a net for a cube, but may not be so sure about the others. There is some evidence to suggest that boys are able to visualise shapes more effectively than girls.

Curriculum links		
KS2	Ma3 2b	Visualise and describe 2D and 3D shapes and the way they behave, making more precise use of geometrical language, especially that of triangles, quadrilaterals, and prisms and pyramids of various kinds; recognise when shapes are identical
KS2	Ma3 2d	Visualise 3D shapes from 2D drawings

5.5 2D representations of 3D objects

Figure 5.4

The error

The child finds it difficult to represent a 3D object as a 2D drawing. They may also find it difficult to recreate a model of blocks from a sketch.

Why this happens

Although the ability to transfer learning from a 2D representation to a 3D representation develops rapidly during childhood (Barr, 2010), young children (and some older people, too) find it very difficult to translate what they see in 3D space to a representation of it on paper, or 2D space. It is sometimes equally difficult to visualise a 3D shape from a 2D drawing. Young children also tend to draw what they think they see, rather than what is presented to them (Picard and Durand, 2004).

Curriculum links		
KS1	Ma3 2c	Create 2D shapes and 3D shapes
KS2	Ma3 1h	Use mathematical reasoning to explain features of shape and space
KS2	Ma3 2c	Make and draw with increasing accuracy 2D and 3D shapes and patterns
KS2	Ma3 2d	Visualise 3D shapes from 2D drawings

5.6 Orientation of two-dimensional shapes

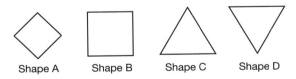

Figure 5.5

The error

The child identifies Shapes A and B as a diamond and a square respectively but does not acknowledge that they are the same shape. Likewise, the child identifies shape C as a triangle, but cannot name shape D.

Why this happens

Children who have been exposed only or mainly to prototypical images of squares or triangles (i.e. shapes with a horizontal baseline) and have not explored them in different rotations will focus on the visual image they have of the shape. This leads to difficulties in identifying the same shape presented in different ways.

Curriculum links		
EYFS		Use language such as 'circle' or 'bigger' to describe the shape and size of solids and flat shapes
KS1	Ma 3 1g	Understand patterns and properties of shape
KS1	Ma3 2a	Describe properties of shapes that they can see or visualise using the related vocabulary
KS1	Ma3 2b	Observe, handle and describe common 2D and 3D shapes; name and describe the mathematical features of common 2D and 3D shapes, including triangles of various kinds, rectangles including squares, circles, cubes, cuboids, then hexagons, pentagons, cylinders, pyramids, cones and spheres
KS2	Ma3 1h	Use mathematical reasoning to explain features of shape and space
KS2	Ma3 2b	Visualise and describe 2D and 3D shapes and the way they behave … recognise when shapes are identical

5.7 Properties of polygons

Example 1: triangles and hexagons

See Figure 5.6.

The error

The child identifies the shapes in Set A as triangles, but cannot name the shapes in Set B as triangles. The child identifies the shapes in Set C as hexagons but does not identify the shapes in Set D as hexagons.

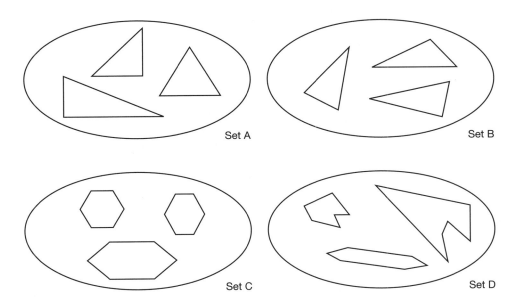

Figure 5.6

Why this happens

Children who have been exposed only or mainly to prototypical images of figures (e.g. triangles with a horizontal baseline, specific examples of right-angled triangles or only equilateral triangles; regular hexagons, hexagons with a horizontal base line or some symmetry) and have not explored them in different rotations will focus on the visual image they have of the shape. This leads to children concluding:

- all triangles have a horizontal baseline;
- only regular (equilateral) triangles are triangles;
- all hexagons have a horizontal baseline;
- only regular six-sided figures are called hexagons.

Example 2: circles

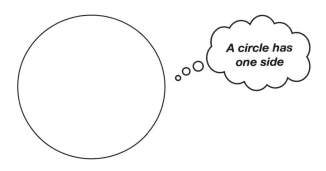

Figure 5.7

The error

The child states that a circle has only one side.

Why this happens

The child can see one side, they draw one (curved) line when they draw a circle and they follow one line when they cut out a circle. In reality, of course, the circle is a *polygon* (*poly* = many, *gon* = sides) with an infinite number of sides (points). There are several ways to define a circle. One commonly accepted definition is a closed plane curve where all points are equidistant (the same distance) from the centre.

Example 3: polygons

Figure 5.8

The error

The child identifies all of these shapes as polygons.

Why this happens

Some children create their own logic from the images they have explored. In this example, the child has been told previously that square, triangle and rectangle are all polygons. She has extrapolated that *other shapes she knows the name of*, such as the heart and the crescent, are polygons. She also extrapolates that as quadrilaterals have four lines, the third shape is also a polygon. She has not yet realised that a polygon must be a closed, plane shape made up of straight lines.

Curriculum links		
For all examples, the curriculum links are as follows.		
EYFS	Use language such as 'circle' or 'bigger' to describe the shape and size of solids and flat shapes	
KS1	Ma 3 1g	Understand patterns and properties of shape
KS1	Ma3 2a	Describe properties of shapes that they can see or visualise using the related vocabulary

KS1	Ma3 2b	Observe, handle and describe common 2D and 3D shapes; name and describe the mathematical features of common 2D and 3D shapes, including triangles of various kinds, rectangles including squares, circles, cubes, cuboids, then hexagons, pentagons, cylinders, pyramids, cones and spheres
KS2	Ma3 1h	Use mathematical reasoning to explain features of shape and space
KS2	Ma3 1h	Use mathematical reasoning to explain features of shape and space
KS2	Ma3 2b	Visualise and describe 2D and 3D shapes and the way they behave ... recognise when shapes are identical
KS2	Ma3 2c	Recognise ... geometrical features and properties including angles, faces, pairs of parallel lines and symmetry, and use these to classify shapes and solve problems

5.8 Right angles

Angle A   Angle B   Angle C

Figure 5.9

The error

The child has identified that angle A is a right angle, but does not recognise angles B or C as right angles.

Why this happens

Children are often presented with prototypical examples of right angles. As a result, they do not recognise other orientations of the angle.

Curriculum links		
KS1	Ma3 3a	Recognise right angles
KS2	Ma3 2a	Recognise right angles, perpendicular and parallel lines; know that angles are measured in degrees and that one whole turn is 360 degrees and angles at a point total 360 degrees, then recognise that angles at a point on a straight line total 180 degrees; know that the sum of the angles of a triangle is 180 degrees

5.9 Parallel and perpendicular lines

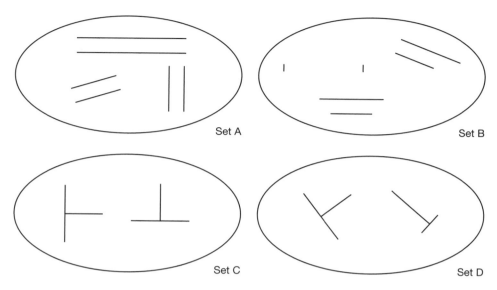

Figure 5.10

The error

The child identifies the shapes in Set A as parallel lines, but does not acknowledge the parallel lines in Set B as parallel lines. Likewise, the child identifies the shapes in Set C as perpendicular lines, but does not acknowledge the lines in Set D as perpendicular lines.

Why this happens

Children who have been exposed only or mainly to prototypical images of parallel or perpendicular lines and have not explored them in different rotations or with lines of varying length will focus on the visual image they have. (Prototypical examples of parallel lines may include lines that are the same length, often running horizontal or vertical with lines longer than the distance between them. Prototypical examples of perpendicular lines usually include lines that are the same length and are horizontal and vertical in orientation.)

Curriculum links		
KS2	Ma3 2a	Recognise right angles, perpendicular and parallel lines; know that angles are measured in degrees and that one whole turn is 360 degrees and angles at a point total 360 degrees, then recognise that angles at a point on a straight line total 180 degrees; know that the sum of the angles of a triangle is 180 degrees

5.10 Definitions of quadrilaterals

Figure 5.11 Parallelograms

The error

The child sees each of the shapes in Figure 5.11 as discrete identities and does not understand that a square is a particular example of a rectangle and that a square and rectangle are particular examples of parallelogram.

Why this happens

Children who have always been shown prototypical shapes of squares, rectangles and parallelograms (such as those above) have not explored the properties of these shapes. They may not have encountered a square as a type of rectangle, for example, as they have always related images of *oblongs* with the label *rectangle*.

This also occurs with other quadrilaterals such as a square being an example of a rhombus and diamonds being examples of kites (see further discussion about kites in Chapter 1).

Curriculum links		
KS2	Ma3 1h	Use mathematical reasoning to explain features of shape and space
KS2	Ma3 2b	Visualise and describe 2D and 3D shapes and the way they behave, making more precise use of geometrical language, especially that of triangles, quadrilaterals, and prisms and pyramids of various kinds; recognise when shapes are identical
KS2	Ma3 2c	Recognise ... geometrical features and properties including angles, faces, pairs of parallel lines and symmetry, and use these to classify shapes and solve problems

Position and direction

In addition to beginning to understand the properties of shapes, at primary level children explore space through positioning themselves, objects and shapes in space. Garrick *et al.* (2004) report that pattern-making is an activity that young children can carry out in order to naturally explore position. Appropriate use of positional language is essential to help children to make sense of position in space and to solve geometrical problems (Greeno, 1980).

Because of the dynamic environments that ICT offers, concepts of position and direction are made more accessible to all children (Jones, 2003). The collaborative nature of the environments also allow for more problem-solving strategies to be used by the children. The following difficulties relate to position and direction.

5.11 Positional language

My teddy is next to the chair!

Figure 5.12

The error

The child uses the incorrect positional vocabulary to explain the position of the teddy.

Why this happens

Children come to school with a wide variation in their spoken language. This is usually dependent on how much talking about position they did prior to attending school, either at home or at nursery. A lack of specific vocabulary may not necessarily mean that a child does not understand an object's position. For example, a child with English as an additional language may already know positional words in their home language(s) but not yet fully understand the English equivalents. A child's inability to solve a geometrical problem can often be traced back to a lack of positional understanding.

Curriculum links		
KS1	Ma3 1d	Use the correct language and vocabulary for shape, space and measures
KS1	Ma3 1e	Recognise simple spatial patterns and relationships and make predictions about them
KS1	Ma3 3a	Observe, visualise and describe positions, directions and movements using common words

5.12 Plotting, reading and writing co-ordinates

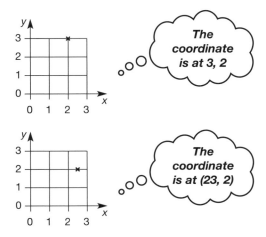

Figure 5.13

The error

The child states that the co-ordinate is at (y, x) rather than at (x, y) or the child finds it difficult to label a co-ordinate that is not at an intersection of two points.

Why this happens

The child does not understand the convention of labelling of co-ordinates according to (x-axis, y-axis). First children are expected to use co-ordinates to label spaces, for example in games like 'Battleships'. Often when this is the case, they will use mixed notation, for example: D2. As the mathematics becomes more sophisticated, there is a need for children to move on to labelling points on lines for accuracy. This parallels children's development on a number track to a number line. A point that does not appear on an intersection requires use and application of decimal and/or measurement (length) knowledge.

Curriculum links		
KS2	Ma2 4e	Read and plot co-ordinates in the first quadrant, then in all four quadrants.
KS2	Ma3 3b	Transform objects in practical situations; transform images using ICT; visualise and predict the position of a shape following a rotation, reflection or translation
KS2	Ma3 3c	Identify and draw 2D shapes in different orientations on grids; locate and draw shapes using co-ordinates in the first quadrant, then in all four quadrants

5.13 Following directions: left and right, compass directions

The error

The child turns left instead of right.

Why this happens

'Left' and 'right' are only labels used to distinguish between two different directions and it is no wonder that children often confuse the two. It takes practice and reinforcement at home and school to perfect the difference. Sometimes, however, the confusion is more than just forgetting which is which. If two children are facing each other, then they will find their left and right hands are on the same side. This is the same when a child is looking in a mirror. It is challenging for children to give instructions to another child, a programmable robot, or Logo turtle, as the child has to place themselves into the other's shoes to ensure the correct command. Similar difficulties are faced by children when they begin to use compass directions: north, south, west, east, northeast, west northwest, and so on.

Curriculum links		
EYFS		Use developing mathematical ideas and methods to solve practical problems
EYFS		Use everyday words to describe position
KS1	Ma3 1d	Use the correct language and vocabulary for shape, space and measures
KS1	Ma3 1e	Recognise simple spatial patterns and relationships and make predictions about them
KS1	Ma3 3b	Recognise movements in a straight line (translations) and rotations, and combine them in simple ways
KS2	Ma3 3a	Visualise and describe movements using appropriate language
KS2	Ma3 3b	Transform objects in practical situations; transform images using ICT; visualise and predict the position of a shape following a rotation, reflection or translation

Transformation

This section is concerned with children's difficulties in the transformation of shape in space. Transformation includes enlargement and aspects of symmetry such as reflection, rotation and translation.

Garrick (2002) considered young children's perceptions of symmetrical patterns. In her research she found that 8% of the 3-year-olds she worked with were able to construct their own pegboard symmetrical patterns. By four years of age, this had significantly increased to 25%. Rawson (1993) looked at the pattern perception of four- to six-year-old children and identified that in several cases the children searched for a visual balance in the manipulatives and were implicitly placing importance on symmetry as a feature of pattern. Clements (2003, page 42) also reports that symmetry is *an area of strength* for young children.

At times it can be useful to consider symmetry as closely linked to fractions. Often teachers consider lines of symmetry as reflecting one-half of a pattern. This can, however, cause difficulties. Huckstep *et al.* (2002) share an example where a teacher inadvertently muddies the symmetrical properties of an oblong to her class when she is looking at halves and quarters of squares and then moves on to oblongs. The children want to halve the oblong diagonally, which then leads the teacher to use rotation to demonstrate how the oblong is cut in half. Another aspect of symmetry is reflecting shapes in one, two or more lines of symmetry.

Orton (1997) carried out a study with older children, from 9 to 16 years of age. These children identified pattern as including 'ideas of shape recognition, congruence and symmetry' (page 304). She found that although the children had a clearly established understanding of pattern recognition, they lacked the vocabulary needed to describe it. Orton identified a three-stage process that children undertake in their understanding of pattern.

Stage 1: copying shapes, detecting embedded shapes in pictures, completing simple patterns, matching shapes, recognising reflection in a vertical line, simple rotation and reflection and completing tasks with a frame of reference.

Stage 2: matching embedded shapes, matching simple shapes in different orientations, undertaking more complex reflection and rotation tasks with a frame of reference.

Stage 3: matching more complex shapes in different orientations, completing more complex tasks involving rotation, recognising most reflection and rotation. (Orton, 1997, page 310).

Children first reflect in one horizontal or vertical line, with the shapes touching the line. The shapes then move a distance from the line and finally the line is set on the diagonal. The order of teaching these reflects the level of difficulty that children experience (Orton, 2004). The importance of mathematical terminology in geometrical understanding has already been highlighted in this chapter. However, once again, the issue of mathematical terminology must be raised. It appears that the importance of vocabulary and the observed lack of use of correct terminology is not limited to children. Goulding (2002) found that trainee teachers were lacking terminology of transformations and she suggested that this may have caused trainees difficulty with their mathematical tasks. It is, of course, vital that teachers model good mathematical terminology to their children.

5.14 Lines of symmetry

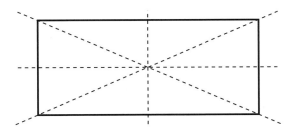

Figure 5.14

The error

The child identifies four lines of symmetry in an oblong.

Why this happens

Often when we discuss reflection with children, we use terms that include referring to 'half', such as *reflect this pattern into the other half* or *find the other half*. This leads children to assume that half of an object is the reflection of it, as in this case where the child has halved the oblong as many times as possible. In addition to this, the two right-angled triangles look similar visually and will in fact rotate around the centre of the oblong to fit onto each other. Identifying the diagonals as lines of symmetry also identifies a lack of understanding of the distance of the perpendicular from the line of symmetry to any point on the shape.

Curriculum links		
KS2	Ma3 1h	Use mathematical reasoning to explain features of shape and space
KS2	Ma3 2c	Recognise reflective symmetry in regular polygons

5.15 Reflection

The following examples are illustrations of misconceptions in reflection.

Example 1: Reflection in a vertical or horizontal line

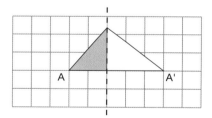

Figure 5.15

The error

The child inaccurately reflects point A.

Why this happens

The child may have simply made an error by miscalculating the distance from the line of symmetry to point A. Alternatively, this may demonstrate a misunderstanding of the need to maintain the length of the sides in the reflection or the need for the perpendicular distance between points and the line of symmetry to be equal.

Example 2: Reflection in a vertical or horizontal line at a distance

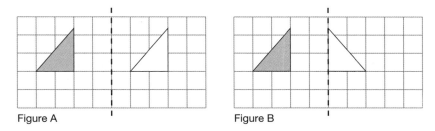

Figure A   Figure B

Figure 5.16

The error

The child inaccurately reflects the shape.

Why this happens

In Figure A, the child may have simply made an error by confusing reflection with translation or, alternatively, this may show a misunderstanding of how the shape changes orientation through reflection. Both figures may show a misunderstanding of how the perpendicular distance between points and the line of symmetry remains the same in a reflection.

Example 3: Reflection in a diagonal line of symmetry

The error

The child inaccurately reflects the shape in the line of symmetry (Figure 5.17).

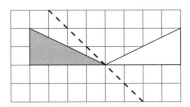

Figure 5.17

Why this happens

Children find reflecting in lines that are not horizontal or vertical a lot more difficult because of the dominant visual pictures they develop through the horizontal and vertical experience they have. These experiences allow children to count the number of squares across and up or down to identify the reflected points. In this example it is likely that the child has found it difficult to reflect in the diagonal, thus treating it as a vertical line of symmetry. It may also demonstrate that the child does not understand that each point in the reflected shape must have the same perpendicular distance from the line of symmetry.

Curriculum links		
KS2	Ma3 1g	Present and interpret solutions to problems
KS2	Ma3 1h	Use mathematical reasoning to explain features of shape and space
KS2	Ma3 3a	Visualise and describe movements using appropriate language
KS2	Ma3 3b	Transform objects in practical situations; transform images using ICT; visualise and predict the position of a shape following a rotation, reflection or translation

5.16 Order of rotation

The following examples illustrate misconceptions related to rotation.

Example 1: order of rotation of regular pentagons

This regular pentagon has an order of rotation of six!

Figure 5.18

See Figure 5.18.

The error

The child believes they have identified the correct order of rotation because they have counted six rotations.

Why this happens

This is usually due to an incorrect counting technique. The child may have begun counting the first order of rotation before rotating it about the centre the first time, or they may have counted an extra rotation at the end as they forgot where they began the rotations. This is more common with regular shapes.

Example 2: rotation around a point

The error

See Figure 5.19. The child translates (Figure 5.19, A) or reflects (Figure 5.19, B) the tile rather than rotating it around the centre of rotation.

Why this happens

Children may apply the techniques they learned when studying translation or reflection earlier. They may also be confused between reflective and rotational symmetry. This could be due to the poor examples that they are asked to complete in class, as some patterns look the same after the initial tile has been reflected or rotated. (See, for example the tiles in example 3 below. These could have been produced by rotation or reflection.) If a child completes a task in this way, they are not demonstrating their knowledge of the need for all points on the tile to be the same distance from the centre of rotation and that the orientation of the tile changes.

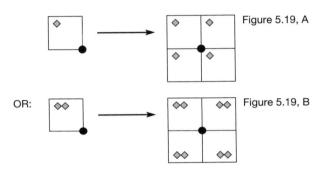

Figure 5.19, A

Figure 5.19, B

Figure 5.19

Example 3: rotation around a point at a distance

The error

The child does not leave the correct distance from the shape being rotated to the centre of rotation (Figure 5.20).

Figure 5.20

Why this happens

Along with reflecting a shape that is a distance from the line of symmetry, rotating around a centre of rotation that is not in contact with the shape is equally difficult for children. Errors often occur if children have not had a lot of experience with rotating shapes some distance from the centre of rotation.

Curriculum links		
KS1	Ma3 3b	Recognise movements in a straight line (translations) and rotations, and combine them in simple ways
KS2	Ma3 3a	Visualise and describe movements using appropriate language
KS2	Ma3 3b	Transform objects in practical situations; transform images using ICT; visualise and predict the position of a shape following a rotation, reflection or translation

5.17 Enlargement

The error

The child believes that when they double the size of a shape, the area will also double

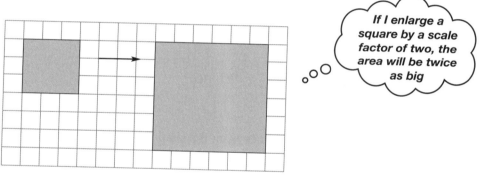

If I enlarge a square by a scale factor of two, the area will be twice as big

Figure 5.21

Why this happens

In number operations, whatever happens to one side of an operation usually happens to the other. Therefore, it is common for children to believe that if they double the length of the sides on a shape, the area will also double.

The error

The child believes that it is impossible to multiply the sides of Square A to make Square B as Square B is smaller and multiplying makes the answer bigger (Figure 5.22).

Why this happens

As in number, there is a common misunderstanding that multiplication always makes numbers bigger. Of course we can enlarge square A by a scale factor of 0.5 to make square B, just as multiplying by a half makes a number half the size. Some teachers confuse children by talking about 'reducing' a shape by half. This demonstrates the conflict between the technical use of the word 'enlargement' and its use in ordinary English which can often be identified in mathematics.

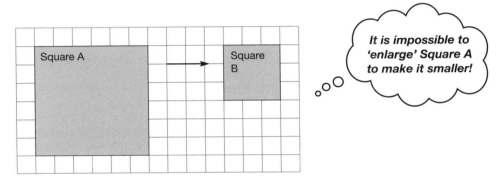

Figure 5.22

Curriculum links		
KS2	Ma2 2h	Solve simple problems involving ratio and direct proportion
KS2	Ma3 3a	Visualise and describe movements using appropriate language
KS2	Ma3 3b	Transform objects in practical situations; transform images using ICT; visualise and predict the position of a shape following a rotation, reflection or translation

5.18 Tessellation

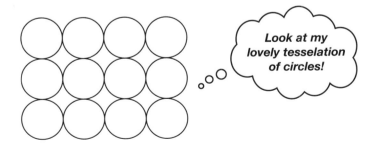

Figure 5.23

The error

The child believes they have tessellated the circles because they have created a repeating pattern.

Why this happens

Tessellation, mathematically speaking, only occurs when the vertices of the shape(s) fit together to meet at 360°. Children often focus on the repeating pattern rather than the properties of the angles where the shapes meet whilst tessellating shapes.

Curriculum links		
KS1	Ma3 3a	Observe, visualise and describe positions, directions and movements using common words
KS2	Ma3 2c	Make and draw with increasing accuracy 2D and 3D shapes and patterns; recognise reflective symmetry in regular polygons; recognise their geometrical features and properties including angles, faces, pairs of parallel lines and symmetry, and use these to classify shapes and solve problems
KS2	Ma3 3b	Transform objects in practical situations; transform images using ICT; visualise and predict the position of a shape following a rotation, reflection

6

Measures

John Dudgeon and Alice Hansen

Chapter overview

Measurement has always played a vital role in helping our society function. It is easy to see that measurement is an extension of number and allows us opportunities to develop skills within that area. However, there is a clear distinction between number and measures. Measurement is a real-life application for number, but number can be abstract. Additionally, a number can be precise, but a measurement will only ever be an approximation to the unit being measured.

Transitivity and *conservation* are principles that relate to all aspects of measurement. Transitivity is an important mathematical principle that measure allows us to address because it enables us to order a set of more than two objects. If we know that box A is heavier than box B and box B is heavier than box C, then box A must be heavier than box C. We have been able to compare boxes A and C through their relations to B. We have allowed box B to act as an intervening measure (Cross *et al.*, 2009, page 359). Logical reasoning, such as transitivity, was shown by Nunes *et al.* (2007) to have a causal link in children's mathematical understanding. They trained children in logical reasoning, and found that they made more mathematical progress than a control group who had not received the training. This demonstrates that children's mathematical development is dependent on them understanding the underlying logic. Earlier, Nunes and Bryant (1996, page 76) explained how *no one can have the slightest idea how a ruler works unless he or she can also make and understand such inferences.*

Piaget identified *conservation* as an ability in logical reasoning. He explained how it is a key indicator to a child's intelligence and is a vital component of the understanding of measurement. Knowing that the volume of water in a tall glass does not change when it is poured into a short glass, or that the two pieces of a torn piece of paper have the same surface area as before, is knowing that the transformation has had no effect on the equivalence. However, around the same time as Piaget's work was being published, Smedslund (1961) researched children's acquisition of conservation of substance and weight. Smedslund's findings challenge Piaget's explanation of conservation acquisition as a process of inner equilibrium and instead suggest that the concepts are more likely to be established through external reinforcement (teaching and learning). Perhaps Castle and Needham's (2007) research offers a way forward. They researched Grade 1 children's understanding of measurement. One key recommendation from their work was that teachers should focus on what it means to measure, rather than focus on how to measure. Teachers need to consider carefully how these key ideas are to be met and how to use the possible misconceptions that arise from these as opportunities to develop their pupils. This is echoed in Clement and Sarama's (2009, page 164) statement that *measuring is a difficult skill, but it also involves many concepts.*

Measurement is inherent in much of the Problem Solving, Reasoning and Numeracy strand of The Statutory Framework for the Early Years Foundation Stage (DCSF, 2007). For example, children are expected to use language such as 'bigger'. Measurement forms part of Attainment Target 3 of the National Curriculum for Mathematics in England (DfEE, 1999b). Key Stage 1 children should be able to compare, estimate and measure different lengths, masses and capacities. They should also be able to read a simple scale, use a ruler to draw and measure lines to the nearest centimetre. Through Key Stage 2, children are introduced to the relationships between units of length, mass and capacity and the use of a protractor to measure angle. They are also taught the concept of area as a measure of square centimetres and how to calculate perimeter.

Length

Length is one of the simpler measures to introduce to children because it is one-dimensional and young children learn notions of direct comparisons early. However, there are many concepts within the notion of linear measurement. These are:

- lengths span fixed distances (attribute);
- as objects move, their fixed length does not change (conservation);
- if A is longer than B, and B is longer then C, then A is longer than C (transitivity);
- an object can be sliced up into smaller sections – this is important to understand when understanding that a measurement, for example 5cm, is not simply a mark on a ruler but can be cut up onto units (equal partitioning);
- the length of a unit is a part of the length of the object being measured – and therefore those units can be placed end on end to identify the length of the object (units and unit iteration);
- as a unit is iterated, the counting word stated on each iteration represents the length covered by all the units (accumulation of distance and additivity);
- any point on a measuring scale can be used as the origin (origin);
- items that are counted refer to continuous units (*relation between number and measurement*).

(adapted from Clements and Sarama, 2009)

If children do not understand these concepts, misconceptions and errors can arise. For example, if the need for a 'baseline' is not understood, objects are not accurately matched and compared.

Piaget (1970) observed children's perception that the length of an object can be altered by a change in position. The concept of conservation (that an object is the same length whatever its orientation) is one that children need many examples of to aid their understanding. Indeed, Barrett and Clements (2003) showed that for children to further their understanding of the concept of linear measurement, they required activities beyond measurement of straight lines. Experience involving tasks such as measuring perimeter and the sides of polygons appeared to promote a more abstract understanding of length.

6.1 Direct comparison of two objects

The teacher gives the child two objects to compare. They place them on the desk as in Figure 6.1.

The grey stick is longer

Figure 6.1

The error

The child has not matched the ends of the objects together giving a false impression of the largest and smallest.

Why this happens

Children sometimes fail to understand that in order to give a fair comparison it is important that two ends are carefully put at the same level. Having little previous experience on which to base a mental comparison, a child's answer can be confused by the position of the objects. The visual image of one object looking longer than the other can be avoided by the use of a line the children could use to match the ends first.

Curriculum links		
EYFS	Use language such as 'greater', 'smaller', 'heavier' or 'lighter' to compare quantities	
KS1	Ma3 4a	Estimate the size of objects and order them by direct comparison using appropriate language

6.2 Comparing a straight line and a crooked line

The teacher draws two lines on the whiteboard, one straight and one crooked (Figure 6.2). The teacher then asks which line is longer.

These must be the same length. They start and finish at the same place

Figure 6.2

The error

The child looks at the lines and decides that they are the same length.

Why this happens

Some children do not realise that a crooked line is longer than a straight line between the same two points. In considering only end points or destination, the points in between do not matter. The child has looked at the two starting points and the two end points and has not visualised the lines in terms of an ordered system of points and intervals.

Curriculum links		
EYFS	Use language such as 'greater', 'smaller', 'heavier' or 'lighter' to compare quantities	
KS1	Ma3 4a	Compare and measure objects using uniform non-standard units, then with a standard unit

6.3 Conservation of length

The practitioner observes a young child's actions and makes a note of their conversation:

Saima held a stick in her hand. I asked her what she noticed about the stick. Holding it vertically, she said, 'It is long, long.' She ran her hand along the stick. I agreed. Then she turned it horizontally and looked at it. I asked what she was thinking. She said, 'It isn't as long now'. I asked, 'Why not?' and Saima said, 'Cos it is longer that way' as she rotated it 90°.

The error

The child thinks that the same stick is longer when it vertical and shorter when it is horizontal.

Why this happens

Saima does not understand the concept of conservation and has not realised that the length of the stick is invariant. She may also be comparing the height of the stick when it is vertical with the height (the stick's width) when it is horizontal.

Curriculum links		
KS1	Ma3 4a	Compare and measure objects using uniform non-standard units, then with a standard unit of length

6.4 Using rulers and tape measures

The teacher gives the class some identical objects to measure (Figures 6.3 a, b, c, d, e).

The error

The children return with lots of different answers even though they were measuring identical objects.

Why this happens

(a) The children start to measure from the edge of the ruler (when zero does not start at the end of the ruler they are using). The children do not understand the *origin* concept.

Figure 6.3a

(b) The children start to measure from 1 cm instead of 0cm. The children do not understand the origin concept. This is a common error because children start counting from one.

Figure 6.3b

(c) The children have read the number from the scale on the other edge of the ruler (or tape measure) when it has scales on both edges (progressing in different directions).

Figure 6.3c

(d) The children have measured the object from the wrong end of the ruler.

Figure 6.3d

(e) In using the tape measures the children have failed to take account of the metal end on some of the tapes given. The children whose tape measures started from the end avoided this error.

Figure 6.3e

(f) The children have failed to mark accurately before moving the ruler/tape measure along when measuring lengths longer than the ruler.

(g) The children have failed to measure in a parallel direction.

Curriculum links		
KS1	Ma3 4c	Estimate, measure and weigh objects; choose and use simple measuring instruments, reading and interpreting numbers, and scales to the nearest labelled division
KS2	Ma3 1a	Recognise the need for standard units of measurement
KS2	Ma3 4b	Recognise that measurement is approximate; choose and use suitable measuring instruments for a task; interpret numbers and read scales with increasing accuracy; record measurements using decimal notation

6.5 Using trundle wheels

The teacher has asked groups of children to measure the perimeter of the playground and playing field. They choose a trundle wheel as the most appropriate piece of equipment to use.

The error

The groups all have different answers on their return.

Why this happens

- Some of the children failed to start the trundle wheel in the correct position. The wheel must start with the 0cm or 0m mark touching the ground before they start to move.
- On moving around the playground, some of the children miscounted the number of clicks made by the wheel.
- When reaching the end of the measurement, the children just counted the clicks and did not account for the fraction of a turn left on the wheel.
- The children made errors in reading the scale itself.
- The children were unable to get the wheel into corners or right up to walls or fences and they did not account for the difference.

Curriculum links		
KS1	Ma3 4c	Estimate, measure and weigh objects; choose and use simple measuring instruments, reading and interpreting numbers, and scales to the nearest labelled division
KS2	Ma3 1a	Recognise the need for standard units of measurement
KS2	Ma3 4b	Recognise that measurement is approximate; choose and use suitable measuring instruments for a task; interpret numbers and read scales with increasing accuracy; record measurements using decimal notation

Area and perimeter

Children as young as six months of age can detect that there is a difference in area representing a 1:2 change in the area (Brannon *et al.*, 2006). However, it is widely accepted that the relationship between area and perimeter is complex (Yeo, 2008).

Area is the quantity of surface within a specified closed boundary. As area is a two-dimensional measure, direct comparison can be very difficult. See Figure 6.4 (Figure A, Figure B).

It is not difficult to see in Figure A which shape has the largest area – we are able to compare visually because we recognise that the shortest sides on both rectangles are the same.

Figure 6.4, A

However, in Figure B the shortest sides on both rectangles are not the same, so the answer is more difficult to work out.

Figure 6.4, B

When we arrive at the problem of comparing irregular shapes, it can become virtually impossible by visual comparison. The difference between one-dimensional and two-dimensional measures when dealing with area also causes confusion when children are asked to look at perimeter, as they both involve looking at the boundary of the shape. Haylock (2001) points out that the relationship between perimeter and area provides us with a counter-example of the principle of conservation. Rearranging an imaginary perimeter fence around a field to change its shape, without changing the overall perimeter, does not conserve the area (see Haylock, 2001, pages 188–90). Yeo (2008) identified that it is difficult for children to understand how two lines (the length and the width) can produce an area when they are multiplied. Indeed, Yeo cites Menon's (1998) research on student teachers' understanding of area and perimeter, where they found that the student teachers have a procedural understanding of area and perimeter rather than a conceptual and relational understanding.

6.6 Conservation of area

The teacher asks the children to cut up a piece of rectangular card and rearrange the pieces to make a different shape (Figure 6.5). A child is then asked if the area of the shape has changed.

Figure 6.5

The error

The child responds by doing the task and replying that the area has changed because the shape has changed.

Why this happens

Children often look at the amount of space a shape takes up and come to the conclusion that the more spread out a shape is, the more area it must take. A parallelogram is often looked at as having a bigger area than a rectangle because it appears to be more spread out.

Curriculum links

KS2	Ma3 4e	Find perimeters of simple shapes; find areas of rectangles using the formula, understanding its connection to counting squares and how it extends this approach; calculate the perimeter and area of shapes composed of rectangles

6.7 The relationship between length and area

The teacher asks the child what would happen to the area of a rectangle if the length and width were doubled (Figure 6.6).

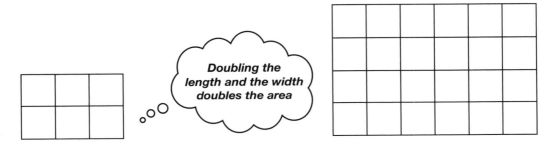

Figure 6.6

The error

The child answers that if you double the width and the length, then the area will be doubled.

Why this happens

The child has incorrectly extrapolated that by multiplying the length of the sides, the same scale factor would apply to the area as was applied to the length and the width.

Curriculum links

KS2	Ma3 4e	Find perimeters of simple shapes; find areas of rectangles using the formula, understanding its connection to counting squares and how it extends this approach; calculate the perimeter and area of shapes composed of rectangles

6.8 Area and perimeter interdependence

The teacher asks the children if changing the perimeter of a shape changes the area (Figure 6.7).

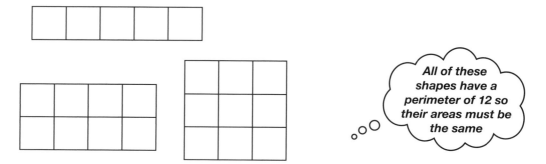

Figure 6.7

The error

The children agree that the shapes have all changed but all have a perimeter of 12 units so the areas must be the same.

Why this happens

The children have not had enough opportunities to realise that changing either the area or the perimeter may or may not cause a change in both cases. There is no direct link or relationship between the changing of area and its effect on the perimeter, and vice versa.

Curriculum links		
KS2	Ma3 4e	Find perimeters of simple shapes; find areas of rectangles using the formula, understanding its connection to counting squares and how it extends this approach; calculate the perimeter and area of shapes composed of rectangles

6.9 Use of inappropriate units

The child is asked to find the area of a rectangle. The child's response is as shown in Figure 6.8.

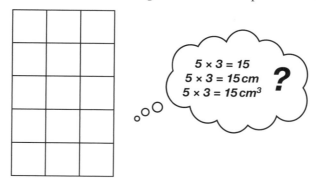

Figure 6.8

The error

The child is unsure which unit to use.

Why this happens

After calculating the area, which is done correctly using the formula required, the child does not understand the importance of answering using the correct units. They are not sure of the need for a unit and this could be indicative of a child's lack of understanding of what they are measuring in the first place.

Curriculum links		
KS2	Ma3 1a	Recognise the need for standard units of measurement
KS2	Ma3 4a	Recognise the need for standard units of length, mass and capacity, choose which ones are suitable for a task, and use them to make sensible estimates in everyday situations
KS2	Ma3 4e	Find perimeters of simple shapes; find areas of rectangles using the formula, understanding its connection to counting squares and how it extends this approach; calculate the perimeter and area of shapes composed of rectangles

Mass and weight

The vocabulary that we use in our everyday lives leads to a confusion about how we teach 'mass' and 'weight'. The scientific and mathematical meanings of the words are not the same as those used by many people. The terms we actually use are inappropriate, as mass is the amount of matter within an object whereas weight is the force of gravity acting upon an object. When we use the word 'weight' we often mean mass and when we say 'weigh' we mean 'find the mass' (Haylock, 2001).

The scales we use cannot measure mass directly, only the force of gravity upon the object we are measuring. This is possible due to the fact that mass and weight are directly proportional. In Key Stage 1 children can be allowed to treat mass and weight as the same, but in Key Stage 2 they will learn the distinction between the two.

Unlike length, mass cannot be appreciated visually, as Haylock and Cockburn (1997) state *you cannot perceive it, count it, smell it or feel it* and, without the use of a balance, direct comparison of the mass of objects is impossible. Early experiences can be acquired through holding items in each hand and comparing them, although it must be remembered the children are experiencing weight, not mass. Children can also find this a problem due to the fact that the area of contact of the object they are holding varies.

Collecting and using a wide range of non-uniform and non-standard units develops the idea of units for mass. These need to be used with a balance, which does compare mass. Using vocabulary that suggests an object has the same mass as 15 pebbles can be progressed through to the same idea using uniform, non-standard units such as multilink, marbles, pennies, etc. When children are introduced to standard units for mass, work can be done on finding items heavier than and lighter than a given mass. Haylock (2001) suggests referring to the standard units we use in the classroom as 'masses' rather than weights.

The *transitivity* principle and the *conservation* principle discussed earlier in this chapter can also cause difficulties for children when dealing with mass and weight. The opportunity to place three or more objects in order using the appropriate type of measure should be frequently offered to the children. Effective questioning when these activities are taking place will help to embed these principles in the children's learning.

6.10 Conservation of mass

The teacher suggests that two balls of modelling clay have the same mass. The child agrees that the two identical balls do indeed have the same mass. The teacher rolls out one of the balls and asks if they both still have the same mass (Figure 6.9).

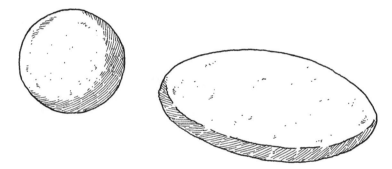

Figure 6.9

The error

The child thinks that because the modelling clay has changed shape, then the mass will have changed.

Why this happens

Children have difficulties with the *conservation* principle. Children often believe that changing the shape of an object will change its mass. This can also be witnessed when children break up a ball of modelling clay into smaller pieces or convert smaller pieces into one large piece. The transformation of the original shape leads some children to believe the total mass must be different.

Curriculum links

KS1	Ma3 4a	Estimate the size of objects and order them by direct comparison using appropriate language; compare and measure objects using uniform non-standard units, then with a standard unit of weight (kg)

KS1	Ma3 4c	Estimate, measure and weigh objects; choose and use simple measuring instruments, reading and interpreting numbers, and scales to the nearest labelled division
KS2	Ma3 1a	Recognise the need for standard units of measurement
KS2	Ma3 4a	Recognise the need for standard units of length, mass and capacity, choose which ones are suitable for a task, and use them to make sensible estimates in everyday situations

6.11 Mass determined by volume

The teacher shows a class of children two boxes: one is very large but light; the other is smaller but heavier (Figure 6.10). The teacher asks the children to decide, just by looking, which is the heavier box.

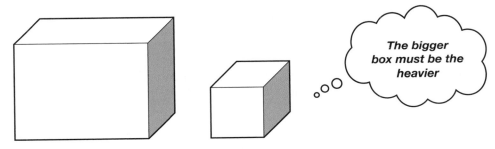

Figure 6.10

The error

The children answer that the bigger box is the heavier.

Why this happens

This comes from the children's belief that the mass of an object is determined from its volume. The bigger an object, the heavier it must be. It is important for the children to realise that visual image does not reflect weight.

Curriculum links		
KS1	Ma3 4a	Estimate the size of objects and order them by direct comparison using appropriate language; compare and measure objects using uniform non-standard units, then with a standard unit of weight (kg)
KS1	Ma3 4c	Estimate, measure and weigh objects; choose and use simple measuring instruments, reading and interpreting numbers, and scales to the nearest labelled division

KS2	Ma3 1a	Recognise the need for standard units of measurement
KS2	Ma3 4a	Recognise the need for standard units of length, mass and capacity, choose which ones are suitable for a task, and use them to make sensible estimates in everyday situations

Volume and capacity

Volume is the third aspect within the logical progression from length (1D), area (2D) and volume (3D) in terms of the amount of space being measured.

Sáiz and Figueras (2009) highlight how confusion between volume and capacity occurs because people tend to use the two terms interchangeably. Additionally, volume was defined three ways by Piaget *et al.* (1970), and Sáiz (2003) identified five meanings from the research literature. Essentially, volume is the amount of 3D space which is occupied by an object. Capacity, on the other hand, can be defined as a measure of the space with which a 3D container can be filled. This distinction is often confused as we talk about interior volume and exterior volume. In the main we tend to use the term 'volume' for shapes that are solid. If we fill something with liquid we then use the term 'capacity' and in Key Stage 1 the term can be used to explore the ability to fill containers (Haylock, 2001). In reality, as internal volume and capacity are measuring the same thing the distinction is not crucial. It becomes crucial, however, when we are referring to the *external* volume or the volume of the material the container is made from.

Sáiz and Figueras (2009) conducted a literature review of the errors and misconceptions that children experience with volume. These include children:

- exhibiting difficulties with 2D representations of 3D objects, particularly if they are required to 'count' cubes that are not visible;
- not distinguishing between weight and volume;
- believing that enlarging the linear measurement of the object x times makes the volume x times larger;
- not distinguishing between volume and capacity;
- not distinguishing between surface area and volume;
- believing that two objects with the same surface area will have the same volume;
- relating the rise of displaced liquid to weight of an object rather than volume.

(adapted from Sáiz and Figueras, 2009, pages 148–9)

Children's vocabulary should be developed through practical tasks involving the use of a range of different- sized containers. Words such as 'full' and 'empty' can be developed into 'holds more' and 'holds less'. Comparisons of containers being filled and emptied (pouring one into another) will enable the children to compare more than two containers. By Year 5, approximately 80% of children will have a good understanding of conservation of liquid (Twidle, 2006), so around one child in five is likely to experience difficulties in the upper primary years. Children need a lot of experience of using a variety of arbitrary units before they realise that comparisons require the same unit. At this point they can move on to deciding the most suitable unit to use and look at standard measuring devices such as beakers and measuring cylinders. It is important that children are aware of the link between capacity and volume to help them with displacement problems. This is a much more difficult concept for children to understand (Twidle, 2006).

Discovering that 1 litre of water has the same volume as 1000 cubic centimetres (and also has a mass of 1kg) is a vital concept for children to grasp. Using centimetre cubes to find the volume of regular shapes also helps develop links between the measurement of volume and capacity.

6.12 Conservation and capacity

The children watch their teacher pour some water from one container into another and are then asked if the amount of water has changed (Figure 6.11).

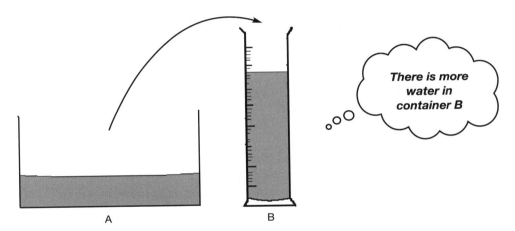

Figure 6.11

The error

It appears that there is more water in the second container. The children believe that the amount of water must have changed.

Why this happens

The children looking at the second container see that the depth of the water has changed and thus the amount of water must have changed. This is a conservation problem. Children often believe that taller containers contain more than shorter containers. The children could also struggle to deal with more than one variable in terms of the height and the cross-section of the containers.

Curriculum links

KS1	Ma3 4a	Estimate the size of objects and order them by direct comparison using appropriate language; compare and measure objects using uniform non-standard units, then with a standard unit of capacity (l)
KS1	Ma3 4c	Estimate, measure and weigh objects; choose and use simple measuring instruments, reading and interpreting numbers, and scales to the nearest labelled division
KS2	Ma3 1a	Recognise the need for standard units of measurement

6.13 Errors when using measuring cylinders

The teacher asks the children to write down the amount of liquid that has been poured into a cylinder (Figures 6.12, A, B, C).

The error

The children write down a range of different answers.

Figure 6.12, A

Why this happens

- Some children pick the cylinder up and then fail to keep it vertical when reading the scale.
- Some children read the scale by looking at the value at the top of the meniscus instead of at the base.

Figure 6.12, B

- Some children read the scale from different heights so that parallax errors occur.
- Some children make errors in reading the scale itself.

Figure 6.12, C

Curriculum links

KS1	Ma3 4c	Estimate, measure and weigh objects; choose and use simple measuring instruments, reading and interpreting numbers, and scales to the nearest labelled division
KS2	Ma3 4b	Recognise that measurement is approximate; choose and use suitable measuring instruments for a task; interpret numbers and read scales with increasing accuracy; record measurements using decimal notation

Time

Children need to understand two aspects of time. Firstly, there is a 'passage of time' (for example, the time taken to run 100m, the time between breakfast and dinner or the time between Christmas and Easter). These time intervals are measured in seconds, minutes, hours, days, weeks and so on. Secondly, there is a 'recorded time' (for example, the time when something happens). For this we use analogue or digital time such as 'o'clock' and the 24-hour system. Neither of these aspects should be taught as isolated topics but need to be raised with the children whenever possible within a variety of cross-curricular contexts (Haylock, 2001). Putting time into meaningful contexts gives children the opportunity to begin to understand cyclical patterns (for example, days of the week, seasons). Using the vocabulary of 'today', 'tomorrow' and 'yesterday' in a story, for example, should complement activities that look at the passage of time.

While time passes at a constant rate, it often doesn't feel like that as a direct experience. Five minutes at the dentist might feel a lot longer than five minutes at a party! Cockburn (1999) uses the analogy of 'a long time for a historian' and 'a long time for a child' when looking at some of the problems in teaching the passing of time. Indeed, no one currently understands how we can psychologically estimate the duration of time (Karmarkar and Buonomano, 2007). Children are often only aware of the recent past or near future and so it is important that early tasks do not incorporate long periods of time.

When starting to learn about the measurement of time (as opposed to the passage of time) it is important to note that telling the time is really a scale-reading task. Hopkins *et al.* (2004) suggest that the dial of an analogue clock is a linear scale wrapped round into a circle. They go on to say that *the complexity of the scale used on the analogue clock is not always recognised* (2004, page 207). Children will go through a process of learning specific times of the day, for instance dinnertime, through recognising hours, parts of the hour, minutes and seconds. Their understanding of time is not helped by the fact that time is not metric and has many different units to get to grips with. There are a number of ways that we can tell the time, for example:

- Twenty-five to nine
- Eight thirty-five
- Twenty-five to nine in the evening
- Eight thirty-five in the evening
- Eight thirty-five p.m.
- Twenty thirty-five

These conventions all add to the confusion – as does the use of phrases like *I won't be a second* or *just a minute*. Not being able to watch the hour hand move also confuses children into thinking that the hour hand and the minute hand move independently.

6.14 Vocabulary related to time

A young child tells her teacher that she went to visit Grandma and Granddad 'yesterday'. The teacher knows that she was at school yesterday and talks with her about how she visited her grandparents last week, rather than yesterday.

The error

The child refers to an event that happened last week but refers to the event happening 'yesterday'.

Why this happens

Children take a long time to be able to understand the passing of time and correctly use language to explain the passing of time or the position of an event in time. It is also possible to observe this when children are talking about the future, confusing, for example 'in a minute', 'tomorrow' with 'next week', 'next month', or 'next year', etc.

Curriculum links		
KS1	Ma3 4a	Compare the durations of events using a standard unit of time

6.15 Analogue clocks

The teacher asks the class what time it is on the classroom clock (Figure 6.13).

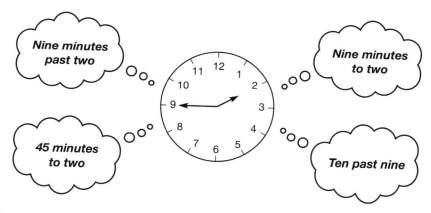

Figure 6.13

The error

The children respond with a range of answers.

Why this happens

- Some of the children misinterpret the hour hand as the minute hand and vice versa. For example, the children may read the clock as 'Ten past nine'.
- Some of the children use the hour numbers on the clock to read the minutes also (i.e. the clock could read 'nine minutes past two' or as 'nine minutes to two').
- The children get confused because we impose two scales – hours and minutes.

- The children make errors when they identify the time between two known values.
- The children get confused about which side of the clock is 'to' the hour and which side is 'past' the hour.
- The children get confused over the use of fractions on an analogue clock. For example, the clock in Figure 6.13 can be read as 'a quarter to two'. In addition to the minutes not being specifically labelled, the fractions of the hours aren't either.

Curriculum links

KS1	Ma3 4a	Compare the durations of events using a standard unit of time
KS2	Ma3 4b	Recognise that measurement is approximate; choose and use suitable measuring instruments for a task; interpret numbers and read scales with increasing accuracy
KS2	Ma3 4d	Read the time from analogue and digital 12- and 24-hour clocks; use units of time – seconds, minutes, hours, days, weeks – and know the relationship between them

6.16 Digital and 24-hour clocks

The teacher asks the class what time it is on the digital clock (Figure 6.14).

Figure 6.14

The error

The children respond with a range of answers.

Why this happens

- Mixing up the hours and the minutes. The children may read the clock in Figure 6.14 as saying 'Eleven minutes past ten'.
- The children can get confused by mixing up digital minutes and decimals. They might read 'ten past eleven' as 'eleven point one'.
- The 12- and 24-hour clock causes confusion without 'p.m.' or 'a.m.' on the digital clock. 'Eighteen forty-five' is unusual language for a child.
- Confusion can arise out of the colloquial use of 'fourteen hundred', which could be expressing the time 14:00. The children can think that the two zeros mean a hundred.

Curriculum links

KS1	Ma3 4a	Compare the durations of events using a standard unit of time
KS2	Ma3 4b	Recognise that measurement is approximate; choose and use suitable measuring instruments for a task; interpret numbers and read scales with increasing accuracy; record measurements using decimal notation
KS2	Ma3 4d	Read the time from analogue and digital 12- and 24-hour clocks; use units of time – seconds, minutes, hours, days, weeks – and know the relationship between them

Angles

Angles can be defined three ways: either as *an amount of turning about a point between two lines; a pair of rays with a common end-point; and the region formed by the intersection of two half-planes* (Mitchelmore and White, 2000). These definitions show us that we can broadly consider the concept of angle in two ways. There is the *static* experience, which focuses on the difference in direction of two lines. This enables us to compare, order and measure the sizes of different angles by placing one on the other or by using a protractor. The second way we can view angles is the *dynamic* experience, which focuses on the rotation involved when one point turns to another. This allows us to appreciate a sense of direction, movement, to look at angles of any size and to distinguish between clockwise and anti-clockwise motion. Providing experiences for children to understand both ways of viewing angles is important for the development of their concept of angles (Clements and Burns, 2005).

Mitchelmore and White (2000) undertook some research which attempted to address children's difficulties in co-ordinating different aspects of the angle concept. They aimed to relate children's angle concepts to their physical experiences. Their research identified three stages of development in children's understanding of angle.

- *Physical angle situations* that young children experience, such as scissors, roundabouts, slides (slope is a way to consider angle), pencil points, flexible drinking straws, etc.
- *Contextual angle concepts*: children by the age of nine tend to have formed clear and distinct contextual angle concepts (slope, turn, intersection, corner)
- *Abstract angle concepts*: children have generalised the contextual angle concepts and identified abstract angle concepts that may not be similar in context (intersection, corner, bend, slope, limited rotation, unlimited rotation)

6.17 Angle size dependent on bounding lines

The teacher asks the children which angle is bigger (Figure 6.15).

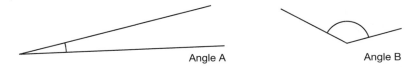

Figure 6.15

The error

The child states that angle A is larger than angle B.

Why this happens

Some children confuse the length of the lines bounding the angle of rotation with the size of the angle. This occurs if a child does not actually understand what the angle is measuring (i.e. the rotation of the lines). Often children are only presented with a static image of angles rather than a balance between those and the dynamic motion that angles can also portray.

Curriculum links		
KS2	Ma3 2a	Recognise right angles, perpendicular and parallel lines; know that angles are measured in degrees
KS2	Ma3 4c	Recognise angles as greater or less than a right angle or half-turn, estimate their size and order them; measure and draw acute, obtuse and right angles to the nearest degree

6.18 Angle size dependent on distance of arc

The teacher asks the child which angle is bigger (Figure 6.16).

Figure 6.16

The error

The child states that angle A is smaller than angle B.

Why this happens

Some children confuse the length of the arc which identifies the angle with the size of the angle. This occurs if a child does not actually understand what the angle is measuring (i.e. the rotation of the lines). Often children are only presented with a static image of angles rather than a balance between those and the dynamic motion that angles can also portray. In this particular example, the angles are the same size; however, the visual impact of the arc has an impact on the child's perspective.

Curriculum links		
KS2	Ma3 2a	Know that angles are measured in degrees
KS2	Ma3 4c	Recognise angles as greater or less than a right angle or half-turn, estimate their size and order them; measure and draw acute, obtuse and right angles to the nearest degree

6.19 Reflex angles

The error

The child states that it is impossible to have an angle greater than 360° because 360° is the largest angle possible.

Why this happens

Children learn that there are 360 degrees in a circle and they are shown many examples of this in their shape and space work. They are also given many opportunities to measure and create angles that are smaller than 360°, so it is understandable that they make the assumption that it is not possible to find an angle larger than that. Given opportunities such as considering how many degrees the big hand of the clock has moved to rotate from one to one and then on to seven helps overcome this. There is also a need for children to see angles as dynamic measurements, rather than just static representations of a measurement.

Curriculum links		
KS2	Ma3 2a	Know that one whole turn is 360 degrees and angles at a point total 360 degrees
KS2	Ma3 4c	Recognise angles as greater or less than a right angle or half-turn, estimate their size and order them; measure and draw acute, obtuse and right angles to the nearest degree

6.20 Errors when using a protractor

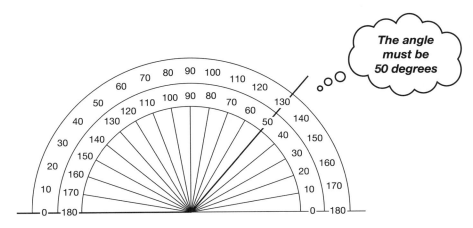

The angle
must be
50 degrees

Figure 6.17

The error

The children provide many different answers.

Why this happens

1 When setting the protractor the children fail to line up the correct lines that make up the angle and so do not start from 0 degrees.

2 The children read the protractor scale but get confused with there being two different scales. They read the one going in the opposite direction to the one they need.

3 The children make errors when they identify the degrees between two known values.

Curriculum links		
KS2	Ma3 2a	Know that angles are measured in degrees
KS2	Ma3 4b	Recognise that measurement is approximate; choose and use suitable measuring instruments for a task; interpret numbers and read scales with increasing accuracy
KS2	Ma3 4c	Recognise angles as greater or less than a right angle or half-turn, estimate their size and order them; measure and draw acute, obtuse and right angles to the nearest degree

7

Handling data

Liz Surtees

Chapter overview

Handling data presents the ideal opportunity to link mathematics to other areas of the curriculum and the real world. Children need to be introduced to the data-handling cycle: pose questions, collect data, represent data, interpret data, and wherever possible begin the cycle by raising questions that relate to a meaningful enquiry. As Nickson (2000, page 87) states, *It is this desire to use real data that motivates the students and makes the study of statistics important to the subject area.* This is supported by Williams and Eastwood (2004, page 117), who add that *Handling data is not simply making lists. It involves analysing the information and often extrapolating the results to reach definite and defined conclusions. This can only be done with real and relevant information however simple it might be.*

For example, in the Key Stage 2 science unit (DfEE/QCA, 1998) that investigates materials with heat-conducting properties ('Which material will provide the best insulation?'), children need to decide how they will collect and represent their data and finally what it tells them in relation to the question originally posed.

The Statutory Framework for the Early Years Foundation Stage (DfES, 2007) requires opportunities for children to sort objects according to their similarities and differences. They also *need to count objects that share a particular property presenting results using pictures, drawings or numerals* (DfES, 2007, page100). In Key Stage 1, 'Processing, representing and interpreting data' is found within Ma2 (Number) in the National Curriculum for Mathematics in England (DfEE, 1999b), Handling data forms Attainment Target 4 of the National Curriculum for Key Stage 2.

During Key Stage 2 this includes interpreting data in tables, charts and graphs, including those generated by a computer. By the end of Key Stage 2, children will be able to calculate the range and average for a set of data. Probability is introduced in the Year 5 and Year 6 teaching programmes.

Posing questions

Few misconceptions explicitly related to posing questions have been identified by research. However, this section highlights that:

- posing questions is crucial to the data-handling process;
- it is difficult for children to pose appropriate questions;
- selecting inappropriate questions leads to errors and misconceptions within the data handling cycle.

Pepperel *et al.* (2009, page 114) stress that *the cycle has various points which mark stages in the process. The first of these is a starting question. This needs to be of relevance and interest to the children. It may need to be framed so that it is clear what data it is appropriate to collect, although this is not always obvious.* Many data-handling activities begin with either the teacher posing a question or the children being given data as part of an exercise from a book or worksheet. Ideally every data-handling exercise should begin with questions developed from children's interest and involvement.

> *The teacher's role so far has been to identify possible starting points and incorporate them into planning. She will need to consider the sort of questions which will provide rich starting points for children's learning. Such questions will not always be neat and focussed.*
>
> (Pepperel *et al.*, 2009, page 116)

However, as Back and Pumfrey (2007) warn, *in schools we often undertake tasks in which we encourage children to collect data about themselves and their friends but the emphasis tends to be on presenting data in a variety of forms such as bar charts or pictograms. Analysis is often confined to identifying the most popular or least popular item. These limitations tend to restrict the interest and variety of the contexts that are explored, and fail to engage children in any significant mathematical thinking.*

These questions may well be related to work they are covering in other curriculum areas and the teacher might suggest an area or topic as a starting point. School councils can also generate interesting lines of enquiry linked with current school issues such as range of break-time activities. (Avoid sensitive issues such as pocket money that could lead to personal problems for some children.) Discussion will then be needed to make the question (or questions) suitably challenging and also practical within the school context. The type of question will determine how the data are collected, represented and analysed. According to Suggate *et al.* (2001, page 232):

> *There should be an established progression of the types of questions tackled throughout the school. In Key Stage 1 they will be fairly simple factual questions, such as the number of brothers and sisters.*

They go on to suggest that:

> *Later some relation between two measurements might be considered, such as the length of a person's hand-span and his height. More complicated questions about opinions and values might be suitable in Year 6.*

7.1 Children asking questions

After a class discussion on different types of toys, the teacher invites the children to suggest questions they might want to investigate. One child asks, *How many toys do I have?*

The error

The child poses a question that is inappropriate because once the toys have been counted the cycle will end, there is nothing to be interpreted.

Why this happens

Young children are *egocentrical thinkers* (Piaget, 1970). They find it difficult to consider situations beyond themselves and, as a result, may not understand how questions need to be considered from a perspective other than their own.

Curriculum links		
KS1	Ma2 5a	Solve a relevant problem by using simple lists, tables and charts to sort, classify and organise information

Collecting data

Once a question has been decided upon, the children will need to discuss how they are going to collect the data. *Using real data in examples for children to work with always used to be problematic. If numbers have to be manipulated without recourse to technology, then it is sensible to, first, keep the numbers simple, preferably whole and, secondly, to keep the number of examples to a minimum. ICT eliminates this problem* (Briggs and Pritchard, 2002, page 5).

The level of input from the teacher will depend on the age and ability of the children and also the intended learning outcomes. Children may learn a great deal from choosing a method that does not result in them being able to answer the question. They should be encouraged to think about why their method didn't work and about alternative methods they might have chosen. Mooney *et al.* (2000, page 105) assert that *It may be necessary to ask questions about how data were collected in order to ascertain possible sources of error and the limitations of the data collection.* Other children may well become demotivated when they realise that they have spent a long time collecting data that they cannot organise in such a way that will allow for interpretation and hence give an answer to their question. Timely teacher intervention, through questioning, should resolve this.

> *The data which they will collect might be obvious in some cases, as in an enquiry centred on the question 'What is your favourite toy?', but less so in others. For example, if children want to investigate ways to improve the lost-property system in school, what will they need to find out? What kinds of information will help? In each case discussion will be necessary, to help children come up with ideas for themselves in the first instance.*
>
> (Pepperel *et al.*, 2009, page 117)

Examples of appropriate questions that can help children's thinking can be found in the National Numeracy Strategy's *Mathematical Vocabulary* booklet (DfEE, 1994, pages 4–6).

Carpenter *et al.* (1993) found that young children use tally marks intuitively when solving problems. However, all too often in the excitement of recording, the accepted recording of tally marks is forgotten and leads to disorganised data that are more likely to cause errors in counting. Children will also need guidance on how to design an appropriate record sheet and record the most appropriate data in the most effective way.

With older children, questionnaires can be used to gather information, where a number of questions are asked relating to the main question. A lot of discussion and guidance will be needed here, together with a small pilot exercise, so that the children produce questions that are unambiguous and result in responses that can be interpreted productively. Thought needs to be given as to who will respond to questionnaires – if they only ask their friends then the sample will be biased. This may not raise any misconceptions related to the outcomes of the research, but needs to be recognised.

As far as possible, children should avoid 'copying out' raw data as this can lead to errors. Thought will also need to be given as to what the children will record. Emergent readers and writers will need boxes to tick and labels may be drawn by the teacher rather than written. Older children may well benefit from working in mixed-ability groups.

Finally, thought needs to be given as to whether a 'free choice' is allowed and whether data need to be grouped. Restricting choice and grouping data lead to information being lost but does allow simpler, and in some cases, possible, interpretation. For example, considering the previous question, if children name the place they most enjoyed visiting, it would be possible to have as many different places as children. Grouping places, for example, home town, home county, home country, Europe and other parts of the world will lead to more manageable data.

7.2 Tally chart

Birds observed in the school grounds on 5 December.

Type of bird	Tally	Frequency (child)	Frequency (correct)
Blackbird	||	2	2
Robin	|	1	1
Sparrow	⊔⊔⊔⊓	5	5
Starling	⊔⊔⊓ ⊔⊔⊓	10	12

The error

The children make five vertical marks before making a diagonal mark on the sixth count. Children then count each group as a 'five'.

Why this happens

The children are familiar with the tally mark notation, but they do not realise that they should only make four vertical marks before making a diagonal mark on the fifth count.

Curriculum links		
KS1	Ma2 1a	Approach problems involving number, and data presented in a variety of forms, in order to identify what they need to do
KS1	Ma2 1e	Use the correct language, symbols and vocabulary associated with number and data
KS1	Ma2 1g	Present results in an organised way
KS1	Ma2 5a	Solve a relevant problem by using simple lists, tables and charts to sort, classify and organise information

Representing data

Graphs, pictures, tables and diagrams can be used to represent data in a mathematical way. *They can also present their findings to the other members of the class, perhaps using digital images in a Microsoft Powerpoint along with the graphs. This is usually very striking and represents a powerful means for children to present the results of their mathematical investigations* (Williams and Eastwood, 2004, page 5).

Graphs can be used to communicate information/data to a wide audience. This is a skill that needs to be used increasingly in our society that has broadening public accessibility to statistics (Ainley and Pratt, 2001). Care has to be taken to use an appropriate form of representation if its intended purpose is not to mislead or confuse. A similar view was expressed by Orton and Frobisher (2005, page 149), who stated that:

Often, data represented graphically are often easier to comprehend than if they were described in words or even tabulated. Sometimes, a graph might even enable us to perceive connections and relationships which are obscured by the quantity of numbers in the original data. In other words, graphs are an important means of communication, and we should obviously be aiming to enable children to communicate clearly, accurately and attractively through graphs.

Mokros and Tinker's (2006) research reported a number of graph-related misconceptions. One of these was children looking at a graph as a picture, rather than as a source of information. It is important to keep in the children's sights the reason for the representation and for the interpretation of the data they collect. This will address some of the potential errors and misconceptions that arise through lack of purposeful understanding of their mathematics tasks.

7.3 Simple way of organising data

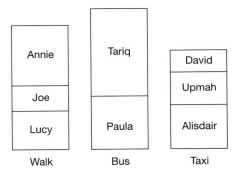

How children travel to school

Figure 7.1

The errors

The children have used inconsistent unit sizes when representing the data in the block graph.

Why this happens

In handling data, we work to many conventions. In this example, the children lack awareness of the need to have units of consistent size. The issue of appropriate scales can be seen in other examples in measures in Chapter 6.

Curriculum links		
KS1	Ma2 5a	Solve a relevant problem by using simple lists, tables and charts to sort, classify and organise information

7.4 Block graphs

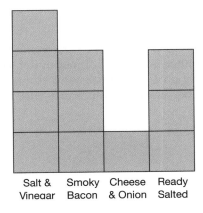

Salt & Vinegar Smoky Bacon Cheese & Onion Ready Salted

Figure 7.2: Favourite crisps

The error

The blocks do not have a gap between columns.

Why this happens

Children do not understand that for discrete data there is no 'connection' between data groups. This is also a common error seen when children draw bar charts. These are often shown incorrectly in textbooks and schemes, i.e. without gaps between the bars.

Curriculum links		
KS1	Ma2 5a	Solve a relevant problem by using simple lists, tables and charts to sort, classify and organise information

7.5 Bar charts: number track used on vertical axis

Figure 7.3

The error

The children have numbered the spaces on the vertical axis of a bar chart.

Why this happens

Children are familiar with number tracks and do not understand that a number line is required. Earlier representation of data used blocks or pictures where each item represented an individual child. This error becomes less common as they become more confident using number lines.

Curriculum links

KS2	Ma4 2c	Represent and interpret discrete data using graphs and diagrams, including pictograms, bar charts and line graphs, then interpret a wider range of graphs and diagrams, using ICT where appropriate

7.6 Bar charts: inconsistent scale used on vertical axis

Figure 7.4

The error

The children have labelled the vertical axis using an inconsistent scale.

Why this happens

Children do not understand that once a scale has been decided upon, e.g. 1cm = 2, all of the axis must be labelled this way. They have chosen only to label the vertical axis with the values they have, 1cm representing different numbers of children.

Curriculum links

KS2	Ma4 2c	Represent and interpret discrete data using graphs and diagrams, including pictograms, bar charts and line graphs, then interpret a wider range of graphs and diagrams, using ICT where appropriate

7.7 Bar charts: inconsistent scale used on horizontal axis

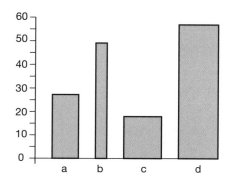

Figure 7.5

The error

The children have used different widths for their bars.

Why this happens

Children do not understand that by convention, we represent data in bar graphs using the same width.

Curriculum links		
KS2	Ma4 2c	Represent and interpret discrete data using graphs and diagrams, including pictograms, bar charts and line graphs, then interpret a wider range of graphs and diagrams, using ICT where appropriate

7.8 Bar charts: incorrect labelling of axis

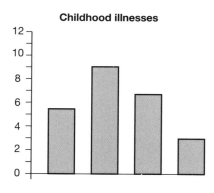

Childhood illnesses

Figure 7.6

The error

The children have not labelled the items represented on the horizontal axis.

Why this happens

Children fail to understand the importance of labelling axes/graphs and so the graph cannot be interpreted by others. This shows a lack of awareness of an intended audience.

This error is not restricted to just the horizontal axis.

Curriculum links		
KS2	Ma4 2c	Represent and interpret discrete data using graphs and diagrams, including pictograms, bar charts and line graphs, then interpret a wider range of graphs and diagrams, using ICT where appropriate

7.9 Bar charts: scale used on vertical axis does not begin at zero

Figure 7.7

The error

Children have labelled the vertical axis starting at 'one'.

Why this happens

Children do not understand that the vertical scale should start at zero, not one. Because children start counting at one, they are confused when labelling the vertical axis. They need to be aware that the axis is a scale of measurement.

Curriculum links		
KS2	Ma4 2c	Represent and interpret discrete data using graphs and diagrams, including pictograms, bar charts and line graphs, then interpret a wider range of graphs and diagrams, using ICT where appropriate

7.10 Bar charts

Crisps	No. of children
Salt & vinegar	12
Cheese & onion	7
Ready salted	3
Smoky bacon	5

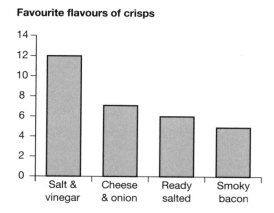

Figure 7.8

The error

Only three children chose ready-salted as their favourite flavour of crisps; however, this is misrepresented in the graph as six children.

Why this happens

Children count the number of lines or squares and ignore the scale.

Curriculum links		
KS2	Ma4 2c	Represent and interpret discrete data using graphs and diagrams, including pictograms, bar charts and line graphs, then interpret a wider range of graphs and diagrams, using ICT where appropriate

7.11 Scatter graph: same scale on both axes

See Figure 7.9.

The error

An inappropriate scale is used on the vertical axis.

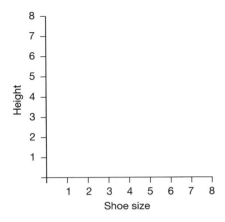

Figure 7.9

Why this happens

The children incorrectly believe that by convention, they must use the same scale on both axes. The children may have also decided to use a scale of 10cm, but omitted this detail when labelling the *y*-axis increments.

Curriculum links		
KS2	Ma4 2c	Represent and interpret discrete data using graphs and diagrams, including pictograms, bar charts and line graphs, then interpret a wider range of graphs and diagrams, using ICT where appropriate

7.12 Misuse of line graphs for discrete data

Shoe size	Y4 frequency	Y5 frequency
2	1	0
3	4	1
4	5	3
5	7	6
6	8	10
7	4	5
8	0	2
9	0	1

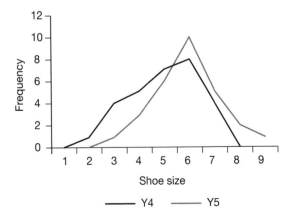

Figure 7.10

The error

The children have represented discrete data as line graphs. They have confused shoe size $(3, 3\frac{1}{2}$, etc.), which is a discrete variable, with the measurement of foot length, a continuous variable.

Why this happens

The chart functions associated with computer spreadsheets allow the user to draw graphs regardless of suitability. In this case discrete data have been represented in a form only appropriate for continuous data.

Curriculum links		
KS2	Ma4 2c	Represent and interpret discrete data using graphs and diagrams, including pictograms, bar charts and line graphs, then interpret a wider range of graphs and diagrams, using ICT where appropriate
KS2	Ma4 2e	Recognise the difference between discrete and continuous data

7.13 Inappropriate representation using pie charts

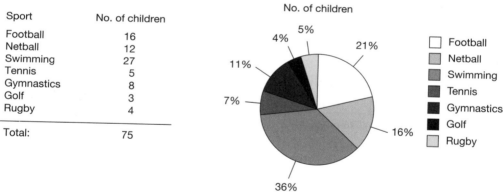

Figure 7.11

The error

The children have inappropriately represented the data in a pie chart.

Why this happens

Children in the class are included more than once, or not at all. A *chart wizard* enables the user to create a variety of charts, some of which may not be appropriate and actually lead to misconceptions.

Curriculum links		
KS2	Ma4 2a	Solve problems involving data
KS2	Ma4 2c	Represent and interpret discrete data using graphs and diagrams, including pictograms, bar charts and line graphs, then interpret a wider range of graphs and diagrams, using ICT where appropriate

7.14 Comparison of pie charts

Number of bedrooms Penrith	Frequency	Number of bedrooms Carlisle	Frequency
1	5	1	13
2	8	2	22
3	30	3	45
4	17	4	53
5	4	5	16
6	1	6	8
7	2	7	5
	—		—
	67		162

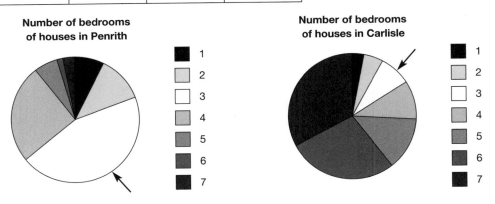

Number of bedrooms of houses in Penrith

Number of bedrooms of houses in Carlisle

The error

The children say that more people live in three-bedroom houses in Penrith than Carlisle.

Why this happens

Children can see that the sector for three-bedroom houses is larger for Penrith than Carlisle. They interpret this as meaning that there are therefore more three-bedroom houses in Penrith. They do not understand that the sector represents a percentage of the total number of houses.

Curriculum links		
KS2	Ma4 2a	Solve problems involving data
KS2	Ma4 2c	Represent and interpret discrete data using graphs and diagrams, including pictograms, bar charts and line graphs, then interpret a wider range of graphs and diagrams, using ICT where appropriate

7.15 Venn diagrams: the intersection

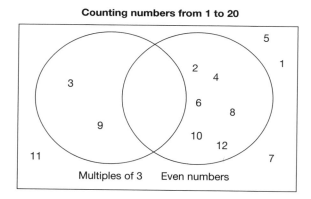

Figure 7.12

The error

The children have not placed 6 and 12 within the intersection of the Venn diagram.

Why this happens

Children do not understand that the intersection of the two sets contains those items of data that fulfil the criteria for both sets.

Curriculum links

| KS1 | Ma2 5a | Solve a relevant problem by using simple lists, tables and charts to sort, classify and organise information |
| KS2 | Ma4 2a | Solve problems involving data |

7.16 Venn diagrams: the universal set

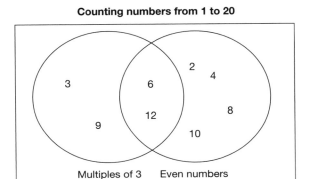

Counting numbers from 1 to 20

Figure 7.13

The error

The children have omitted 1, 5, 7, 11 from the Venn diagram.

Why this happens

Children do not understand that numbers that are not members of either of the two sets need to be placed within the universal set.

Curriculum links

| KS1 | Ma2 5a | Solve a relevant problem by using simple lists, tables and charts to sort, classify and organise information |
| KS2 | Ma4 2a | Solve problems involving data |

7.17 First-stage binary sorting: Carroll diagram

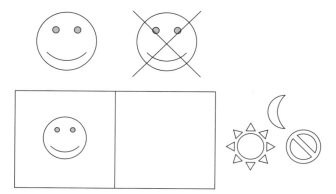

Figure 7.14

The error

The children do not know where to place the shapes that are sun, moon or wheel.

Why this happens

Children do not understand *negation*, that sun/moon/wheel are 'not face'.

Curriculum links		
KS1	Ma2 5a	Solve a relevant problem by using simple lists, tables and charts to sort, classify and organise information
KS2	Ma4 2a	Solve problems involving data

7.18 Second-stage binary sorting: Carroll diagram

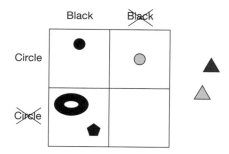

Figure 7.15

The error

The children do not know where to place the triangular shapes that are not black.

Why this happens

The children may not have understood the notion of *negation*, that the other colours are 'not black' and a triangle is 'not a circle'.

Curriculum links		
KS1	Ma2 5a	Solve a relevant problem by using simple lists, tables and charts to sort, classify and organise information

Interpreting data/making deductions

In many classrooms the representation of data falls at the end of the data handling investigation with the initial question being left unanswered. Teachers need to remind children that they are only part way through the data handling cycle.

The interpretation of data is critical, as stated earlier. For children to be motivated, data handling needs a purpose. Assuming the topic chosen for investigation has a purpose then it is necessary to answer any questions posed. Teachers need to allow time for this to happen and scaffold their thinking. An extended plenary session might provide the ideal opportunity. The process is shown in Figure 7.16.

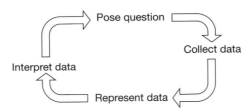

Figure 7.16

It may be even more meaningful for pupils, however, if the interpretive aspect is developed more, so that through discussion and collaboration, the subjective nature of pupils' interpretations will become more obvious. Misconceptions need to be identified before they can be put right and discussion can play a role in this.

(Nickson, 2000, page 107)

With younger children a series of closed questions might be asked, for example, *Which type of rubbish did we collect most of?* With older children this may well lead to open questions such as, *Why do you think Year 5 threw away less paper than Year 4?* All children should be prompted to ask their own questions, both of their own data and of others. Not only will this support their mathematical understanding, it will also provide opportunity for children to reveal (and for you to support/address) further misconceptions about handling data. Although the children may be able to answer the question they posed, it is likely that through discussion more questions will be raised. As Whitin and Whitin say, *by voicing her puzzlement aloud, the teacher demonstrated the importance of checking for reasonableness* (2003, page 147). In some cases, the question or data collection may have been inappropriate, or the graphs drawn misleading.

> *...teachers should give their students opportunities to revise graphs. Revising statistical information enables children to read beyond the data by posing new questions for the class to consider.*

(Couco, 2001, page 147)

In such cases discussion will arise as to what went wrong and how things could be done differently next time. Before they leave primary school, children need to begin to look critically at the data they have collected and consideration needs to be given as to the 'fairness' of their sample. They need to be asked whether the deductions they have made are reliable – a questionnaire full of biased questions is unlikely to lead to this. There is a need to apply intelligence and common sense to all interpretation of data; it is easy to 'jump to conclusions'. As Nickson (2000, page 93) says, *pupils may confuse conditionality and causality. There is a difference between the probability of having measles when a rash appears and the probability of having a rash because one has measles. Having a rash does not depend upon having measles. On the other hand, measles does cause having a rash.*

7.19 Correlation

The children investigate scores in spelling tests within their class. A child produces the graph shown in Figure 7.17.

Height (cm)	Spelling score
130	12
132	14
136	14
138	15
140	16
142	18
144	22
148	24
152	24
155	26

A graph showing our spelling scores and our heights

Figure 7.17

The error

The children say that tall children do better in spelling tests.

Why this happens

The children have concluded that since the majority of high marks scored in spelling tests are gained by children who are taller, then there must be a relationship between two variables. Those children who score highly in spelling tests may be taller than average or vice versa but one variable does not necessarily cause the other.

Curriculum links		
KS2	Ma4 2c	Represent and interpret discrete data using graphs and diagrams, including pictograms, bar charts and line graphs, then interpret a wider range of graphs and diagrams, using ICT where appropriate

7.20 Measure of average: mean

Children are asked to calculate the mean of the following numbers: 5, 6, 7, 2, 7, 9.

The error

Some children accept that the answer is 28.5.

Why this happens

The children have used a scientific calculator to calculate their answer. They do not realise that a scientific calculator uses algebraic logic (BODMAS) and therefore will divide the last number, 9, by the number of items in the sample, 6, before adding the remaining numbers. They also do not understand that the mean must lie within the range of values given. They have not checked that the *solution is reasonable in the context of the problem* (DfEE, 1999b, page 73) and have merely followed the rule to calculate the mean.

Curriculum links		
KS2	Ma4 1e	Check results and ensure that solutions are reasonable in the context of the problem
KS2	Ma4 1d	Select and use appropriate calculation skills to solve problems involving data
KS2	Ma4 2a	Solve problems involving data

7.21 Measure of average: median

Children are asked to calculate the median of the following heights: 134cm, 156cm, 133cm, 142cm, 147cm.

The error

Some children say that the answer is 133cm.

Why this happens

The children have remembered that in order to find the median of a set of data they must select the middle value. They have not understood the importance of putting the values in numerical order first. They have not considered whether or not their solution is reasonable.

Curriculum links		
KS2	Ma4 1d	Select and use appropriate calculation skills to solve problems involving data
KS2	Ma4 1e	Check results and ensure that solutions are reasonable in the context of the problem

7.22 Measure of average: mode and mean

Children are asked to calculate the mode of the following shoe sizes: 5, 6, 7, 4, 7, 9, 7, 4, 5.

The error

Some children say that the answer is 6.

Why this happens

The children have confused mode and mean, finding the sum of all the values and dividing the answer by nine rather than looking for the most frequently occurring value.

Curriculum links		
KS2	Ma4 2d	Know that mode is a measure of average and that range is a measure of spread, and to use both ideas to describe data sets

7.23 Measure of average: mode

Children are asked to calculate the mode of the following shoe sizes: 5, 6, 7, 2, 7, 9, 7, 4, 5.

The error

Some children say that the answer is 3.

Why this happens

The children have realised that there are more size 7s than any other size and that there are three of them. This has formed the basis for their answer. They have not understood that the mode is always one of the values of the variable and is used to represent all the data.

Curriculum links		
KS2	Ma4 2d	Know that mode is a measure of average and that range is a measure of spread, and to use both ideas to describe data sets

7.24 Measure of spread: range

Children are asked to find the range of the following numbers: 5, 6, 7, 2, 7, 9.

The error

Some children say that the answer is 2 to 9.

Why this happens

The children have used their own understanding of the word 'range' (and applied it correctly) rather than applying the mathematical term, i.e. $9 - 2 = 7$.

Curriculum links		
KS2	Ma4 2d	Know that mode is a measure of average and that range is a measure of spread, and to use both ideas to describe data sets

Probability

Although the computation of probabilities can appear to be simple work with fractions, students must grapple with many conceptual challenges in order to understand probability. Misconceptions about probability have been held not only by many students but also by many adults (Konold 1989). To correct misconceptions, it is useful for students to make predictions and then compare the predictions with actual outcomes.

(NCTM, 2000)

Although probability is often taught in the later primary years, clearly opportunities for younger children to be introduced to ideas of uncertainty and chance exist. Many children believe that because something usually happens, it will definitely happen. For example, *I usually have chips for tea, therefore I will definitely have chips tonight*. Children and adults also base decisions incorrectly on intuition. Pepperell *et al.* (2009, page 139) give the example:

'When I go to the supermarket the other queues always move faster than mine' 'It isn't fair to have to get a six to start a game because it's harder to get a six.'

English (2006, page 81) recognises the importance of pupils developing *their understanding of probability through practical activities involving flicking coins, rolling dice, picking counters from bag and so on.* However, as upper Key Stage 2 children *need to appreciate the distinction between experimental and theoretical probability*, this becomes impractical. *Teachers and pupils have more pressing things to do in mathematical lessons than flick coins or roll dice 1,000 times! This is where a spreadsheet can take over, by simulating practical probability experiments using random numbers.*

School visits, journeys to and from school, books and breaktime fruit can all provide possible starting points for discussion. For example, *When the next box of fruit arrives, what might be in it?; Look at the front cover of this book, what do you think it is about?* Physical education provides opportunities for discussing chance: *Who is more likely to win, the red team or the blue team?; Who is most likely to score the first goal?*

Older children need to be introduced to a variety of different games that they can play and then discuss whether or not they are fair.

Fisher alleges that:

> *Pupils have an innate sense of probability. Play 'fair' and 'unfair' games and this will become apparent. For example, put 20 red counters in a bag and 5 blue counters. One pupil is red, the other blue and the winning colour drawn out of a bag gets a Smartie. With such lofty prizes the pupil who is blue soon voices their dissent!*

(Fisher, 2001, page 17)

7.25 Theoretical probability

The children are asked to calculate the probability that the spinner will land on an even number (Figure 7.18).

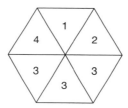

Figure 7.18

The error

Some children say that it is $\frac{1}{2}$.

Why this happens

The children have concluded that since there are four distinct numbers, of which two are even, that the probability must be $\frac{2}{4}$ or $\frac{1}{2}$. They have not realised that there are six equally likely outcomes of which two are even.

Curriculum links		
KS2	Ma4 2f	Draw conclusions from statistics and graphs and recognise when information is presented in a misleading way; explore doubt and certainty and develop an understanding of probability through classroom situations; discuss events using a vocabulary that includes the words 'equally likely', 'fair', 'unfair', 'certain'

7.26 Experimental versus theoretical probability

A fair coin is thrown ten times and on each occasion it lands heads-up. The children are asked what the probability is of the coin showing another head on the next throw. (A fair coin is one where there is an equal chance of it landing on a head or a tail.)

The error

The children say that it will (a) definitely land heads-up on the next throw, or (b) definitely land tails-up on the next throw.

Why this happens

The children may be basing their answers on experimental results rather than equally likely outcomes. As a result, they may believe that a head cannot be thrown twice (or three, etc.) times in a row, therefore believing they can predict the next throw.

Curriculum links		
KS2	Ma4 2f	Draw conclusions from statistics and graphs and recognise when information is presented in a misleading way; explore doubt and certainty and develop an understanding of probability through classroom situations; discuss events using a vocabulary that includes the words 'equally likely', 'fair', 'unfair', 'certain'

Appendix: Curriculum objectives

This Appendix provides a list of objectives that are related to the errors found in Chapters 3-7. You will find objectives from the Statutory Framework for the Early Years Foundation Stage (on this page), National Curriculum objectives (pages 147–157), and objectives from the 2006 Revised Primary Framework for Mathematics (pages 158–177). The referencing uses a numerical code, $x.y$, where x is the chapter, and y is the number of the error in the chapter. Although a comprehensive book, some objectives are not listed here. This means that no errors directly associated with those objectives are listed in this edition. However, please note that you may observe errors or misconceptions related to those objectives. You may wish to speak to your tutors or school-based mentors about these.

STATUTORY FRAMEWORK FOR THE EARLY YEARS FOUNDATION STAGE EARLY LEARNING GOALS	POSSIBLE ERRORS
Problem-solving, reasoning and number	
Say and use number names in order in familiar contexts	3.1
Count reliably up to ten everyday objects	3.2; 3.2; 3.3
Recognise numerals 1 to 9	3.4
Use developing mathematical ideas and methods to solve practical problems	3.9; 3.22; 5.1; 5.13
In practical activities and discussion, begin to use the vocabulary involved in adding and subtracting	4.13; 4.14
Use language such as 'more' or 'less' to compare two numbers	3.3
Begin to relate addition to combining two groups of objects and subtraction to 'taking away'	3.2; 4.13
Use language such as 'greater', 'smaller', 'heavier' or 'lighter' to compare quantities	3.3; 6.1; 6.2
Talk about, recognise and recreate simple patterns	3.22
Use language such as 'circle' or 'bigger' to describe the shape and size of solids and flat shapes	5.1; 5.6
Use everyday words to describe position	5.1; 5.13

NATIONAL CURRICULUM OBJECTIVES	POSSIBLE ERRORS
KEY STAGE 1	
Ma 2 Number	
Using and applying number	
1. Pupils should be taught to:	
Problem-solving	
a) approach problems involving number, and data presented in a variety of forms, in order to identify what they need to do	4.5; 7.2
c) make decisions about which operations and problem-solving strategies to use	4.5; 4.6; 4.21
Communicating	
e) use the correct language, symbols and vocabulary associated with number and data	3.3; 3.4; 3.5; 3.6; 3.7; 3.15; 4.12; 4.13; 4.14; 4.16; 4.17; 4.18; 7.2
f) communicate in spoken, pictorial and written form, at first using informal language and recording, then mathematical language and symbols	3.4; 3.5; 3.6; 3.7; 3.8; 4.5; 4.13; 4.14
Reasoning	
g) present results in an organised way	4.5; 7.2
i) explain their methods and reasoning when solving problems involving number and data	3.22
Numbers and the number system	
2. Pupils should be taught to:	
Counting	
a) count reliably up to 20 objects at first and recognise that if the objects are rearranged the number stays the same; be familiar with the numbers 11 to 20; gradually extend counting to 100 and beyond	3.1; 3.2; 3.3; 4.6; 4.15
Number patterns and sequences	
b) create and describe number patterns; explore and record patterns related to addition and subtraction, and then patterns of multiples of 2, 5 and 10 explaining the patterns and using them to make predictions; recognise sequences, including odd and even numbers to 30 then beyond; recognise the relationship between halving and doubling	3.22; 3.23

NATIONAL CURRICULUM OBJECTIVES	POSSIBLE ERRORS
KEY STAGE 1	
Ma 2 Number	
The number system	
c) read and write numbers to 20 at first and then to 100 or beyond; understand and use the vocabulary of comparing and ordering these numbers; recognise that the position of a digit gives its value and know what each digit represents, including zero as a place holder; order a set of one- and two-digit numbers and position them on a number line and hundred-square; round any two-digit number to the nearest 10	3.4; 3.6; 3.7; 3.8; 4.2
Calculations	
3. Pupils should be taught to:	
Number operations and the relationships between them	
a) understand addition and use related vocabulary; recognise that addition can be done in any order; understand subtraction as both 'take away' and 'difference' and use the related vocabulary; recognise that subtraction is the inverse of addition; give the subtraction corresponding to an addition and vice versa; use the symbol '=' to represent equality; solve simple missing number problems [for example, $6 = 2 + ?$]	4.13; 4.14; 4.15; 4.16; 4.17
Solving numerical problems	
4. Pupils should be taught to:	
a) choose sensible calculation methods to solve whole-number problems (including problems involving money or measures), drawing on their understanding of the operations	3.9; 3.10; 4.17; 4.21
b) check that their answers are reasonable and explain their methods or reasoning.	4.21
Processing, representing and interpreting data	
5. Pupils should be taught to:	
a) solve a relevant problem by using simple lists, tables and charts to sort, classify and organise information	7.1; 7.2; 7.3; 7.4; 7.15; 7.16; 7.17; 7.18

NATIONAL CURRICULUM OBJECTIVES	POSSIBLE ERRORS
KEY STAGE 1	
Ma 3 Shape, space and measures	
Using and applying shape, space and measures	
1. Pupils should be taught to:	
Problem-solving	
a) try different approaches and find ways of overcoming difficulties when solving shape and space problems	5.1
c) select and use appropriate equipment and materials when solving shape and space problems	5.1
Communicating	
d) use the correct language and vocabulary for shape, space and measures	5.11; 5.13
Reasoning	
e) recognise simple spatial patterns and relationships and make predictions about them	3.22; 5.11; 5.13
g) understand patterns and properties of shape	5.6; 5.7
Understanding patterns and properties of shape	
2. Pupils should be taught to:	
a) describe properties of shapes that they can see or visualise using the related vocabulary	5.1; 5.2; 5.3; 5.6; 5.7
b) observe, handle and describe common 2D and 3D shapes; name and describe the mathematical features of common 2D and 3D shapes, including triangles of various kinds, rectangles including squares, circles, cubes, cuboids, then hexagons, pentagons, cylinders, pyramids, cones and spheres	5.1; 5.2; 5.3; 5.6; 5.7
c) create 2D shapes and 3D shapes	5.1; 5.5

NATIONAL CURRICULUM OBJECTIVES	POSSIBLE ERRORS
KEY STAGE 1	
Ma 3 Shape, space and measures	
Understanding properties of position and movement	
3. Pupils should be taught to:	
a) observe, visualise and describe positions, directions and movements using common words	5.11; 5.18
b) recognise movements in a straight line (translations) and rotations, and combine them in simple ways [for example, give instructions to get to the head teacher's office or for rotating a programmable toy]	5.16; 5.13
c) recognise right angles.	5.8
Understanding measures	
4. Pupils should be taught to:	
a) estimate the size of objects and order them by direct comparison using appropriate language; put familiar events in chronological order; compare and measure objects using uniform non-standard units [for example, a straw, wooden cubes], then with a standard unit of length (cm, m), weight (kg), capacity (l) [for example, 'longer or shorter than a metre rule', 'three-and-a-bit litre jugs']; compare the durations of events using a standard unit of time	6.1; 6.2; 6.3; 6.10; 6.11; 6.12; 6.14; 6.15; 6.16
c) estimate, measure and weigh objects; choose and use simple measuring instruments, reading and interpreting numbers, and scales to the nearest labelled division.	6.4; 6.5; 6.10; 6.11; 6.12; 6.13

NATIONAL CURRICULUM OBJECTIVES	POSSIBLE ERRORS
KEY STAGE 2	
Ma 2 Number	
Using and applying number	
1. Pupils should be taught to:	
Problem solving	
a) make connections in mathematics and appreciate the need to use numerical skills and knowledge when solving problems in other parts of the mathematics curriculum	3.17; 3.20; 4.12
b) break down a more complex problem or calculation into simpler steps before attempting a solution; identify the information needed to carry out the tasks	4.21
e) make mental estimates of the answers to calculations; check results	3.17; 4.9; 4.18; 4.19; 4.20
Communicating	
g) use notation diagrams and symbols correctly within a given problem	3.17; 4.16; 4.17
h) present and interpret solutions in the context of the problem	3.11; 4.5; 4.16
i) communicate mathematically, including the use of precise mathematical language	3.5; 3.15; 3.19; 4.4; 4.12; 4.13; 4.14
Reasoning	
j) understand and investigate general statements [for example, 'there are four prime numbers less than 10', 'wrist size is half neck size']	3.21; 4.2
k) search for pattern in their results; develop logical thinking and explain their reasoning.	3.23; 4.2; 4.3; 4.5
Numbers and the number system	
2. Pupils should be taught to:	
Counting	
a) count on and back in tens or hundreds from any two- or three-digit number; recognise and continue number sequences formed by counting on or back in steps of constant size from any integer, extending to negative integers when counting back	3.23

NATIONAL CURRICULUM OBJECTIVES	POSSIBLE ERRORS
KEY STAGE 2	
Ma 2 Number	
Number patterns and sequences	
b) recognise and describe number patterns, including two- and three-digit multiples of 2, 5 or 10, recognising their patterns and using these to make predictions; make general statements, using words to describe a functional relationship, and test these; recognise prime numbers to 20 and square numbers up to 10 × 10; find factor pairs and all the prime factors of any two-digit integer	3.23; 4.22
Integers	
c) read, write and order whole numbers, recognising that the position of a digit gives its value; use correctly the symbols <, >, =; multiply and divide any integer by 10 or 100 then extend to multiplying and dividing by 1000; round integers to the nearest 10 or 100 and then 1000; order a set of negative integers, explaining methods and reasoning; multiply and divide decimals by 10 or 100	3.4; 3.6; 3.7; 4.3
Fractions, percentages and ratio	
d) understand unit fractions [for example, one-third or one-eighth] then fractions that are several parts of one whole [for example, two-thirds or five-eighths], locate them on a number line and use them to find fractions of shapes and quantities	3.12; 3.13; 3.14; 3.15; 3.16; 4.6; 4.7; 4.8
e) understand simple equivalent fractions and simplify fractions by cancelling common factors; compare and order simple fractions by converting them to fractions with a common denominator, explaining their methods and reasoning	3.16; 4.7
f) recognise the equivalence between the decimal and fraction forms of one-half, quarters, tenths and hundredths; understand that 'percentage' means the 'number of parts per 100' and that it can be used for comparisons; find percentages of whole number quantities, using a calculator where appropriate	3.20; 4.11
g) recognise approximate proportions of a whole and use simple fractions and percentages to describe them, explaining their methods and reasoning	3.12; 3.13; 3.21
h) solve simple problems involving ratio and direct proportion	3.21; 4.12; 4.22; 5.17

NATIONAL CURRICULUM OBJECTIVES	POSSIBLE ERRORS
KEY STAGE 2	
Ma 2 Number	
Decimals	
i) understand and use decimal notation for tenths and hundredths in context [for example, order amounts of money, round a sum of money to the nearest £, convert a length such as 1.36 metres to centimetres and vice versa]; locate on a number line, and order, a set of numbers or measurements; then recognise thousandths (only in metric measurements)	3.11; 3.17; 3.18; 4.2; 4.3; 4.9; 4.10
j) round a number with one or two decimal places to the nearest integer or tenth; convert between centimetres and millimetres or metres, then between millimetres and metres, and metres and kilometres, explaining methods and reasoning	4.2
Calculations	
3. Pupils should be taught to:	
Number operations and the relationships between them	
a) develop further their understanding of the four number operations and the relationships between them including inverses; use the related vocabulary; choose suitable number operations to solve a given problem, and recognise similar problems to which they apply	4.1; 4.2; 4.3; 4.13; 4.14; 4.16; 4.17; 4.18; 4.19
Mental methods	
c) work out what they need to add to any two-digit number to make 100, then add or subtract any pair of two-digit whole numbers; handle particular cases of three-digit and four-digit additions and subtractions by using compensation or other methods [for example, 3000 − 1997, 4560 + 998]	4.1
d) recall multiplication facts to 10 × 10 and use them to derive quickly the corresponding division facts	4.2
f) multiply and divide, at first in the range 1 to 100 [for example, 27 × 3, 65 ÷ 5], then for particular cases of larger numbers by using factors, distribution or other methods	4.2; 4.3
Written methods	
g) use written methods to add and subtract positive integers less than 1000, then up to 10,000, then add and subtract numbers involving decimals; use approximations and other strategies to check that their answers are reasonable	4.18; 4.19; 4.20

NATIONAL CURRICULUM OBJECTIVES	POSSIBLE ERRORS
KEY STAGE 2	
Ma 2 Number	
Written methods	
h) use written methods for short multiplication and division by a single-digit integer of two-digit then three-digit then four-digit integers, then of numbers with decimals; then use long multiplication, at first for two-digit by two-digit integer calculations, then for three-digit by two-digit calculations; extend division to informal methods of dividing by a two-digit divisor [for example, 64 ÷ 16]; use approximations and other strategies to check that their answers are reasonable	3.17; 4.4; 4.18; 4.19; 4.20
Calculator methods	
i) use a calculator for calculations involving several digits, including decimals; use a calculator to solve number problems [for example, 4? × 7 = 343]; know how to enter and interpret money calculations and fractions; know how to select the correct key sequence for calculations with more than one operation [for example, 56 × (87 − 48)]	3.11
Solving numerical problems	
4. Pupils should be taught to:	
a) choose, use and combine any of the four number operations to solve word problems involving numbers in 'real life', money or measures of length, mass, capacity or time, then perimeter and area	3.17; 4.5; 4.21
b) choose and use an appropriate way to calculate and explain their methods and reasoning	4.12; 4.14; 4.18; 4.19; 4.20; 4.21
c) estimate answers by approximating and checking that their results are reasonable by thinking about the context of the problem, and where necessary checking accuracy [for example, by using the inverse operation, by repeating the calculation in a different order]	4.7; 4.8; 4.9; 4.19; 4.20; 4.21
d) recognise, represent and interpret simple number relationships, constructing and using formulae in words then symbols [for example, c = 15 n is the cost, in pence, of n articles at 15p each]	4.22
e) read and plot co-ordinates in the first quadrant, then in all four quadrants [for example, plot the vertices of a rectangle, or a graph of the multiples of 3]	5.12

NATIONAL CURRICULUM OBJECTIVES	POSSIBLE ERRORS
KEY STAGE 2	
Ma 3 Shape, space and measures	
Using and applying shape, space and measures	
1. Pupils should be taught to:	
Problem-solving	
a) recognise the need for standard units of measurement	6.4; 6.5; 6.9; 6.10; 6.11; 6.12
Communicating	
g) present and interpret solutions to problems	5.15
Reasoning	
h) use mathematical reasoning to explain features of shape and space	5.5; 5.6; 5.7; 5.10; 5.14; 5.15
Understanding properties of shape	
2. Pupils should be taught to:	
a) recognise right angles, perpendicular and parallel lines; know that angles are measured in degrees and that one whole turn is 360 degrees and angles at a point total 360 degrees, then recognise that angles at a point on a straight line total 180 degrees; know that the sum of the angles of a triangle is 180 degrees	5.8; 5.9; 6.17; 6.18; 6.19; 6.20; 6.21
b) visualise and describe 2D and 3D shapes and the way they behave, making more precise use of geometrical language, especially that of triangles, quadrilaterals, and prisms and pyramids of various kinds; recognise when shapes are identical	5.2; 5.3; 5.4; 5.6; 5.7; 5.9; 5.10; 5.13
c) make and draw with increasing accuracy 2D and 3D shapes and patterns; recognise reflective symmetry in regular polygons; recognise their geometrical features and properties including angles, faces, pairs of parallel lines and symmetry, and use these to classify shapes and solve problems	5.5; 5.7; 5.10; 5.14; 5.18
d) visualise 3D shapes from 2D drawings	5.4; 5.5

NATIONAL CURRICULUM OBJECTIVES	POSSIBLE ERRORS
KEY STAGE 2	
Ma 3 Shape, space and measures	
Understanding properties of position and movement	
3. Pupils should be taught to:	
a) visualise and describe movements using appropriate language	5.13; 5.15; 5.16; 5.17
b) transform objects in practical situations; transform images using ICT; visualise and predict the position of a shape following a rotation, reflection or translation	5.12; 5.13; 5.15; 5.16; 5.17; 5.18
c) identify and draw 2D shapes in different orientations on grids; locate and draw shapes using co-ordinates in the first quadrant, then in all four quadrants [for example, use co-ordinates to locate position in a computer game]	5.12
Understanding measures	
4. Pupils should be taught to:	
a) recognise the need for standard units of length, mass and capacity, choose which ones are suitable for a task, and use them to make sensible estimates in everyday situations; convert one metric unit to another [for example, convert 3.17kg to 3170g] ; know the rough metric equivalents of imperial units still in daily use	6.9; 6.10; 6.11
b) recognise that measurement is approximate; choose and use suitable measuring instruments for a task; interpret numbers and read scales with increasing accuracy; record measurements using decimal notation	6.4; 6.5; 6.13; 6.15; 6.16; 6.20
c) recognise angles as greater or less than a right angle or half-turn, estimate their size and order them; measure and draw acute, obtuse and right angles to the nearest degree	6.17; 6.18; 6.19; 6.20
d) read the time from analogue and digital 12- and 24-hour clocks; use units of time – seconds, minutes, hours, days, weeks – and know the relationship between them	3.19; 6.15; 6.16
e) find perimeters of simple shapes; find areas of rectangles using the formula, understanding its connection to counting squares and how it extends this approach; calculate the perimeter and area of shapes composed of rectangles.	6.6; 6.7; 6.8; 6.9

NATIONAL CURRICULUM OBJECTIVES	POSSIBLE ERRORS
KEY STAGE 2	
Ma 4 Handling data	
Using and applying handling data	
1. Pupils should be taught to:	
Problem-solving	
d) select and use appropriate calculation skills to solve problems involving data	7.20; 7.21
e) check results and ensure that solutions are reasonable in the context of the problem	7.20; 7.21
Processing, representing and interpreting data	
2. Pupils should be taught to:	
a) solve problems involving data	5.17; 5.18; 7.15; 7.16; 7.17; 7.18; 7.20
c) represent and interpret discrete data using graphs and diagrams, including pictograms, bar charts and line graphs, then interpret a wider range of graphs and diagrams, using ICT where appropriate	7.5; 7.6; 7.7; 7.8; 7.9; 7.10; 7.11; 7.12; 7.13; 7.14; 7.19
d) know that mode is a measure of average and that range is a measure of spread, and to use both ideas to describe data sets	7.22; 7.23; 7.24
e) recognise the difference between discrete and continuous data	7.12
f) draw conclusions from statistics and graphs and recognise when information is presented in a misleading way; explore doubt and certainty and develop an understanding of probability through classroom situations; discuss events using a vocabulary that includes the words 'equally likely', 'fair', 'unfair', 'certain'.	7.25; 7.26

PRIMARY FRAMEWORK FOR MATHEMATICS (REVISED 2006)	POSSIBLE ERRORS
USING AND APPLYING MATHEMATICS	
Foundation Stage	
Use developing mathematical, ideas and methods to solve practical problems	
Match sets of objects to numerals that represent the number of objects	3.9; 3.10
Sort objects, making choices and justifying decisions	3.9; 3.10
Talk about, recognise and recreate simple patterns	3.22
Describe solutions to practical problems, drawing on experience, talking about own ideas, methods and choices	3.9; 3.10
Year 1	
Solve problems involving counting, adding, subtracting, doubling or halving in the context of numbers, measures or money; recognise the value of coins	3.1; 4.13; 4.15; 4.16
Describe a problem using numbers, practical materials and diagrams; use these to solve the problem and set the solution back in the original context	4.21
Answer a question by selecting and using suitable equipment, and sorting information, shapes or objects; display results using tables and pictures	4.17
Describe simple patterns and relationships involving numbers or shapes; decide whether examples satisfy given conditions	3.22
Describe ways of solving problems and explain choices and decisions orally or using pictures	4.5
Year 2	
Solve problems involving addition, subtraction, multiplication or division in contexts of numbers, measures or pounds and pence	3.18; 4.13; 4.5
Identify and record the number sentences involved in a problem, carry out the calculations and check that the solution makes sense in the context of the problem	3.18; 4.15; 4.16; 4.17; 4.18; 4.19; 4.20
Follow a line of enquiry; answer questions by selecting and using suitable equipment and information, and organising and presenting the information in lists, tables and simple diagrams	7.1; 7.2; 7.3; 7.4; 7.5; 7.6; 7.7; 7.8; 7.9; 7.10
Describe patterns and relationships involving numbers or shapes, make predictions and test these with examples	3.22; 3.23
Present solutions to problems in an organised way; explain decisions, methods and results in spoken, pictorial and written form, using mathematical language and symbols	4.18; 4.19; 4.20

PRIMARY FRAMEWORK FOR MATHEMATICS (REVISED 2006)	POSSIBLE ERRORS
USING AND APPLYING MATHEMATICS	
Year 3	
Solve one- and two-step problems involving numbers, money or measures, including time, choosing and carrying out appropriate calculations	3.18; 3.19; 4.5; 4.21
Represent the information in a problem using numbers and images; use these to find a solution and present it in context, where appropriate using £.p notation or units of measure	3.17
Follow a line of enquiry by deciding what information is important; make and use lists, tables and graphs to organise and interpret the information	7.1; 7.2; 7.3; 7.4; 7.5; 7.6; 7.7; 7.8; 7.9; 7.10
Use patterns, properties of and relationships between numbers or shapes to identify similarities and differences, and to solve puzzles	3.18; 3.22; 3.23
Describe and explain methods, choices and solutions to problems, orally and in writing, using pictures and diagrams	4.18; 4.19; 4.20
Year 4	
Solve one- and two-step problems involving numbers, money or measures, including time; choose and carry out appropriate calculations, using calculator methods where appropriate	3.17; 3.19; 4.5; 4.21
Represent a problem using number sentences and diagrams, use these to find a strategy to solve the problem and present the solution in the context of the problem	3.17; 4.5
Suggest a line of enquiry and the strategy needed to pursue it; collect, organise and interpret selected information to find answers	7.1; 7.2; 7.3; 7.4; 7.5; 7.6; 7.7; 7.8; 7.9; 7.10
Use knowledge of numbers and shapes to identify patterns, properties and relationships, and apply them to unfamiliar situations; investigate a statement involving numbers and test it with examples	3.2

PRIMARY FRAMEWORK FOR MATHEMATICS (REVISED 2006)	POSSIBLE ERRORS
USING AND APPLYING MATHEMATICS	
Year 5	
Solve one- and two-step problems involving whole numbers and decimals and all four operations, choosing and using appropriate methods, including calculator use	3.17; 3.19; 4.5; 4.21
Represent a problem by identifying and recording the calculations needed to solve it; find possible solutions and confirm them in the context of the problem	3.17; 4.5
Plan and pursue an enquiry; present evidence by collecting, organising and interpreting information; suggest extensions to the enquiry	7.1; 7.2; 7.3; 7.4; 7.5; 7.6; 7.7; 7.8; 7.9; 7.10
Explore patterns, properties and relationships and propose a general statement involving numbers or shapes; identify examples for which the statement is true or false	3.23; 4.22
Year 6	
Solve multi-step problems, and problems involving fractions, decimals and percentages, choosing and using appropriate and efficient methods at each stage, including calculator use	3.11; 3.17; 4.5; 4.21
Represent a problem by identifying and recording the calculations needed to solve it, using symbols for unknown quantities where appropriate; set solutions in the original context and check their accuracy	3.11; 4.5
Suggest, plan and develop lines of enquiry; collect, organise and represent information, interpret results and review methods; identify and answer related questions	7.1; 7.2; 7.3; 7.4; 7.5; 7.6; 7.7; 7.8; 7.9; 7.10; 7.11; 7.12; 7.13; 7.14
Recognise and use sequences, patterns and relationships involving numbers and shapes; suggest hypotheses and test them systematically	3.23; 4.22
Explain reasoning and conclusions, using symbols where appropriate	4.22

PRIMARY FRAMEWORK FOR MATHEMATICS (REVISED 2006)	POSSIBLE ERRORS
USING AND APPLYING MATHEMATICS	
Year 6 progression into Year 7	
Solve numerical problems, present, interpret and compare solutions in the context of the problem	4.21
Interpret and use simple formulae from mathematics and other subjects; represent numbers in a problem with symbols, construct and solve simple linear equations and set the solution back in the context of the problem	4.22
Develop and evaluate lines of enquiry; identify, collect, organise and analyse relevant information; decide how best to represent conclusions and what further questions to ask	7.1; 7.2; 7.3; 7.4; 7.5; 7.6; 7.7; 7.8; 7.9; 7.10; 7.11; 7.12; 7.13; 7.14
Generate sequences and describe the general term in simple cases; use letters and symbols to represent unknown numbers or variables; find counter-examples to disprove a conjecture	3.23; 4.22
Use step-by-step deductions to solve problems involving properties of shapes; explain and justify reasoning and conclusions	5.15; 5.16; 5.17

PRIMARY FRAMEWORK FOR MATHEMATICS (REVISED 2006)	POSSIBLE ERRORS
COUNTING AND UNDERSTANDING NUMBER	
Foundation Stage	
Say and use the number names in order in familiar contexts	3.1
Know that numbers identify how many objects are in a set	3.1; 3.2; 3.3
Count reliably up to ten everyday objects	3.1; 3.2; 3.3
Estimate how many objects they can see and check by counting	3.1; 3.2; 3.3
Count aloud in ones, twos, fives or tens	3.1; 3.2
Use language such as 'more' or 'less' to compare two numbers	3.3
Recognise numerals 1–9	3.4
Year 1	
Count reliably at least 20 objects recognising that when rearranged the number of objects stays the same; relate addition to counting on and count on or back in ones, twos, fives and tens; estimate a number of objects that can be checked by counting	3.1; 3.2; 3.3
Compare and order numbers, using the related vocabulary; use the equals (=) sign	3.3
Read and write numerals, numbers from 0 to at least 20 and the multiples of 10, and position these numbers on a number track and number line	3.4
Use the vocabulary of halves and quarters in context	3.12; 3.13; 3.15
Year 2	
Read and write two- and three-digit numbers in figures and words; describe and extend number sequences and recognise odd and even numbers	3.4
Count up to 100 objects by grouping them and counting in tens, fives or twos; explain what each digit in a two-digit number represents, including numbers where 0 is a place holder; partition two-digit numbers in different ways, including into multiples of ten and one	3.4; 3.5; 3.6; 3.7
Order two-digit numbers and position them on a number line; use the greater than (>), less than (<) signs	3.6
Find one-half, one-quarter and three-quarters of shapes and sets of objects	3.12; 3.13

PRIMARY FRAMEWORK FOR MATHEMATICS (REVISED 2006)	POSSIBLE ERRORS
COUNTING AND UNDERSTANDING NUMBER	
Year 3	
Read, write and order whole numbers to at least 1000 and position them on a number line; count them on a number line; count on from and back to zero in single-digit or multiples of 10	3.2; 3.6; 3.7
Partition three-digit numbers into multiples of 100, 10 and 1 in different ways	3.7
Read and write proper fractions, e.g. $\frac{3}{7}$, $\frac{9}{10}$, interpreting the denominator as the parts of a whole and the numerator as the number of parts; identify fractions of shapes and use diagrams to compare fractions and establish equivalents	3.12; 3.13; 3.14; 3.16; 3.18
Year 4	
Recognise and continue number sequences formed by counting on or back in steps of constant size	3.23
Partition, round and order four-digit whole numbers; use positive and negative numbers in context and position them on a number line; state inequalities using the symbols < and >, e.g. –3 > –5, –1 < +1	3.8; 3.18
Use decimal notation for tenths and hundredths and partition decimals; relate the notation to money and measurement; position one- and two-place decimals on a number line	3.8; 3.11
Use diagrams to identify equivalent fractions, e.g. $\frac{6}{8}$ and $\frac{3}{4}$, or $\frac{70}{100}$ and $\frac{7}{10}$; interpret mixed numbers and position them on a number line, e.g. $3\frac{1}{2}$	3.14; 3.16
Use the vocabulary of ratio and proportion to describe the relationship between two quantities, e.g. 2 to every 3, and between part and whole, e.g. 2 in every 5; estimate proportion, e.g. 'for every 1 red car there are about 4 silver cars', or 'I'm asleep for about $\frac{1}{3}$ of the day'	3.21; 4.6

PRIMARY FRAMEWORK FOR MATHEMATICS (REVISED 2006)	POSSIBLE ERRORS
COUNTING AND UNDERSTANDING NUMBER	
Year 5	
Count from any given number in whole number steps and decimal number steps, extending beyond zero when counting backwards; relate the numbers to their position on a number line	3.23
Explain what each digit represents in whole numbers and numbers with up to two decimal places, and partition these numbers	3.7; 3.8; 3.11; 3.18
Express a smaller whole number as a fraction of a larger one; find equivalent fractions; relate fractions to their decimal representations	3.14; 3.16
Understand percentage as the number of parts in every 100 and express tenths and hundredths as percentages	3.20; 4.11
Use sequences to scale numbers up or down; solve problems involving proportions of quantities and measurements, e.g. decrease quantities in a recipe designed to feed six people	3.21; 4.6
Year 6	
Use decimal notation for tenths, hundredths and thousandths, partition and order numbers with up to three decimal places, and position them on the number line	3.8; 3.11; 3.18
Express a larger whole number as a fraction of a smaller one; simplify fractions; order a set of fractions by converting them to fractions with a common denominator	3.14; 3.16
Express one quantity as a percentage of another, e.g. express £400 as a percentage of £1000; find equivalent percentages, decimals and fractions	3.20; 4.11
Solve simple problems involving direct proportion by scaling quantities up or down	3.21; 4.6
Year 6 progression to Year 7	
Compare and order integers and decimals in different contexts	3.11
Order a set of fractions by converting them to decimals	
Recognise approximate proportions of a whole and use fractions and percentages to describe and compare them, e.g. when interpreting pie charts	3.20; 4.11
Use ratio notation, reduce a ratio to its simplest form and divide a quantity into two parts in a given ratio; solve simple problems involving ratio and direct proportion	3.21; 4.6; 4.12

PRIMARY FRAMEWORK FOR MATHEMATICS (REVISED 2006)	POSSIBLE ERRORS
KNOWING AND USING NUMBER FACTS	
Foundation Stage	
Select two groups of objects to make a given total of objects	3.2
Year 1	
Use knowledge of counting in twos, fives and tens to derive the multiples of 2, 5 and 10 to the tenth multiple	3.23
Year 2	
Derive and recall all addition and subtraction facts for each number to at least 10, all pairs with totals to 20 and all pairs of multiples of 10 with totals up to 100	4.15; 4.16
Understand that halving is the inverse of doubling and derive and recall doubles of all numbers to 20, and the corresponding halves	4.17
Derive and recall multiplication facts for the 2, 5 and 10 times tables and the related division facts; recognise multiples of 2, 5 and 10	4.2; 4.3
Year 3	
Derive and recall all addition and subtraction facts for each number to 20, sums and differences of multiples of 10 and number pairs that total 100	4.15; 4.16
Derive and recall multiplication facts for the 2, 3, 4, 5, 6 and 10 times tables and the corresponding division facts	4.2; 4.3
Year 4	
Derive and recall multiplication facts up to 10×10, the corresponding division facts and multiples of numbers to 10 up to the tenth multiple	4.2; 4.3
Identify pairs of fractions that total 1	4.7
Year 5	
Use knowledge of place value and addition and subtraction of two-digit numbers to derive sums and differences, doubles and halves of decimals, e.g. 6.5 ± 2.7, halve 5.6, double 0.34	4.9; 4.10
Recall quickly multiplication facts up to 10×10, use to multiply pairs of multiples of 10 and 100 and derive quickly corresponding division facts	4.2; 4.3

PRIMARY FRAMEWORK FOR MATHEMATICS (REVISED 2006)	POSSIBLE ERRORS
KNOWING AND USING NUMBER FACTS	
Year 6	
Use knowledge of place value and multiplication facts to 10×10 to derive related multiplication and division facts involving decimal numbers, e.g. 0.8×7, $4.8 \div 6$	4.2; 4.3; 4.9; 4.10
Year 6 progression to Year 7	
Consolidate the rapid recall of number facts, including multiplication facts to 10×10 and the associated division facts	4.2; 4.3

PRIMARY FRAMEWORK FOR MATHEMATICS (REVISED 2006)	POSSIBLE ERRORS
CALCULATING	
Foundation Stage	
Begin to relate addition to combining two groups of objects and subtraction to 'taking away'	4.13
In practical activities and discussion begin to use the vocabulary involved in adding and subtracting	4.13; 4.14
Count repeated groups of the same size	3.1
Year 1	
Relate addition to counting on; recognise that addition can be done in any order; use practical and informal written methods to support the addition of a one-digit number or a multiple of 10 to a one-digit number or a multiple of 10 to a one-digit or two-digit number	4.15; 4.16
Understand subtraction as 'take away' and find a 'difference' by counting up; use practical and informal written methods to support the subtraction of a one-digit number from a one-digit or two-digit number and multiple of 10 from a two-digit number	4.13; 4.14; 4.15
Use the vocabulary related to addition and subtraction and symbols to describe and record addition and subtraction number sentences	4.13; 4.14; 4.15
Year 2	
Add or subtract mentally a one-digit number or a multiple of 10 to or from any two-digit number; use practical and informal written methods to add and subtract two-digit numbers	4.15; 4.16
Understand that subtraction is the inverse of addition and vice versa; use this to derive and record related addition and subtraction number sentences	4.15
Represent repeated addition and arrays as multiplication, and sharing and repeated subtraction (grouping) as division; use practical and informal written methods and related vocabulary to support multiplication and division calculations, including those with remainders	4.8; 4.10
Use the symbols $+$, $-$, $\times$, $\div$ and $=$ to record and interpret number sentences involving all four operations; calculate the value of an unknown in a number sentence, e.g. $30 - \square = 24$, $\square \div 2 = 6$	4.15; 4.16

PRIMARY FRAMEWORK FOR MATHEMATICS (REVISED 2006)	POSSIBLE ERRORS
CALCULATING	
Year 3	
Develop and use written methods to record, support or explain the addition and subtraction of two-digit and three-digit numbers	4.1; 4.16; 4.18; 4.19; 4.20
Multiply one-digit and two-digit numbers by 10 or 100, and describe the effect	4.10
Use practical and informal written methods to multiply and divide two-digit numbers (e.g. 13×3, $30 \div 4$); round remainders up or down, depending on the context	4.15; 4.16
Find unit fractions of numbers and quantities, e.g. $\frac{1}{2}, \frac{1}{3}, \frac{1}{4}$ and $\frac{1}{6}$ of 12 litres	3.13
Year 4	
Add or subtract mentally pairs of two-digit whole numbers, e.g. $47 + 58$, $91 - 35$	4.1
Refine and use the efficient written methods to add and subtract two-digit and three-digit whole numbers and calculations with £.p	3.17; 4.5
Multiply or divide numbers to 1000 by 10 and then 100 (whole-number answers), understanding the effect; relate to scaling up or down	4.2; 4.3
Develop and use written methods to record, support and explain multiplication and division of two-digit numbers by a one-digit number, to include division with remainders, e.g. 15×9, $98 \div 6$	4.4; 4.18; 4.19; 4.20
Find fractions of numbers, quantities or shapes, e.g. $\frac{1}{3}$ of 30 plums, $\frac{3}{8}$ of a 6 by 4 rectangle	3.13
Use a calculator to carry out one- and two-step calculations involving all four operations; recognise negative numbers in the display, correct mistaken entries and interpret the display correctly in the context of money	3.11

PRIMARY FRAMEWORK FOR MATHEMATICS (REVISED 2006)	POSSIBLE ERRORS
CALCULATING	
Year 5	
Use efficient written methods to add and subtract whole numbers and decimals with up to two places	3.17; 4.1; 4.9
Use understanding of place value to multiply and divide whole numbers and decimals by 10, 100 or 1000	4.2; 4.3
Refine and use efficient written methods to multiply and divide HTU × U, U.t × U, TU × TU and HTU ÷ U	4.4; 4.18; 4.19; 4.20
Find fractions using division, e.g. $\frac{1}{100}$ of 5kg, and percentages of numbers and quantities, e.g. 10%, 5% and 15% of £80	3.13
Use a calculator to solve problems, including those involving decimals or fractions, e.g. to find $\frac{3}{4}$ of 150g; interpret the display correctly in the context of measurement	3.11
Year 6	
Use efficient written methods to add and subtract integers and decimals, to multiply and divide integers and decimals by a one-digit integer, and to multiply two-digit and three-digit integers by a two-digit integer	3.17; 4.4; 4.18; 4.19; 4.20
Relate fractions to multiplication and division; express a quotient as a fraction or decimal; find fractions and percentages of whole-number quantities	3.13
Use a calculator to solve problems involving multi-step calculations	3.11; 4.21
Year 6 progression to Year 7	
Consolidate and extend mental methods of calculation to include decimals, fractions and percentages	3.17
Use standard column procedures to add and subtract integers and decimals, and to multiply two-digit and three-digit integers by a one-digit or two-digit integer; extend division to dividing three-digit integers by a two-digit integer	4.4; 4.18; 4.19; 4.20
Calculate percentage increases or decreases and fractions of quantities and measurements (whole-number answers)	4.11; 4.12

PRIMARY FRAMEWORK FOR MATHEMATICS (REVISED 2006)	POSSIBLE ERRORS
UNDERSTANDING SHAPE	
Foundation Stage	
Use familiar objects and common shapes to create and recreate patterns and build models	5.1
Use everyday words to describe position	5.11
Year 1	
Visualise and name common 2D shapes and 3D solids and describe their features; use them to make patterns, pictures and models	5.7
Identify objects that turn about a point (e.g. scissors) or about a line (e.g. a door); recognise and make whole, half and quarter turns	5.8; 5.13; 6.19
Visualise and describe the position of objects and direction and distance when moving them, e.g. when placing or moving objects on a games board	5.11
Year 2	
Visualise common 2D shapes and 3D solids and identify them from pictures of them in different positions and orientations; sort, make and describe shapes, referring to their properties	5.5; 5.7
Identify reflective symmetry in patterns and 2D shapes and draw lines of symmetry in shapes	5.14; 5.15
Follow and give instructions involving position, direction and movement	5.11; 5.13
Recognise and use whole, half and quarter turns, both clockwise and anti-clockwise; know that a right angle represents a quarter turn	5.8
Year 3	
Relate 2D shapes and 3D solids to drawings of them, and describe, classify, draw and make the shapes	5.2; 5.3; 5.5
Draw and complete shapes with reflective symmetry; draw the reflection of a shape in a mirror line along one side	5.11; 5.13
Read and record the vocabulary of position, direction and movement, using the four compass directions to describe movement about a grid	5.12; 5.13
Use a set-square to draw right angles and to identify right angles in 2D shapes; compare angles with a right angle; recognise that a straight line is equivalent to two right angles	5.8; 6.17; 6.18

PRIMARY FRAMEWORK FOR MATHEMATICS (REVISED 2006)	POSSIBLE ERRORS
UNDERSTANDING SHAPE	
Year 4	
Draw polygons and classify them by identifying their properties, including their line symmetry	5.2; 5.3; 5.5; 5.6; 5.7
Visualise 3D objects from 2D drawings; make nets of common solids	5.4
Recognise horizontal and vertical lines; use the eight compass points to describe direction; describe and identify the position of a square on a grid of squares	5.13
Know that angles are measured in degrees and that one whole turn is 360°; compare and order angles less than 180°	6.17; 6.18; 6.19
Year 5	
Identify, visualise and describe properties of rectangles, triangles, regular polygons and 3D solids; use knowledge of properties to draw 2D shapes and identify and draw nets of 3D shapes	5.2; 5.3; 5.6; 5.7; 5.10
Read and plot co-ordinates in the first quadrant and recognise parallel and perpendicular lines in grids and shapes; use a set-square and ruler to draw perpendicular and parallel lines	5.12; 5.9
Complete patterns with up to two lines of symmetry and draw the position of a shape after a reflection or translation	5.14; 5.15; 5.17; 5.18
Estimate, draw and measure acute and obtuse angles using an angle measurer or protractor to a suitable degree of accuracy; calculate angles in a straight line	6.17; 6.18; 6.19; 6.20
Year 6	
Describe, identify and visualise parallel and perpendicular edges or faces; use these properties to classify 2-D shapes and 3D solids	5.7; 5.9; 5.10
Make and draw shapes with increasing accuracy and apply knowledge of their properties	6.20
Visualise and draw on grids of different types where a shape will be after reflection, after translations or after rotation through 90° or 180° about its centre or one of its vertices	5.14; 5.15; 5.16; 5.18
Use co-ordinates in the first quadrant to draw, locate and complete shapes that meet given properties	5.12; 5.17

PRIMARY FRAMEWORK FOR MATHEMATICS (REVISED 2006)	POSSIBLE ERRORS
UNDERSTANDING SHAPE	
Year 6	
Use a protractor to estimate, measure and draw angles, on their own and in shapes; calculate angles in a triangle or around a point	6.20
Year 6 progression to Year 7	
Extend knowledge of properties of triangles and quadrilaterals and use these to solve problems, explaining reasoning with diagrams	5.7; 5.10; 5.17
Use all four quadrants to find co-ordinates of points determined by geometric information	5.12
Identify all the symmetries of 2D shapes; transform images using ICT	5.14; 5.15; 5.16
Construct a triangle given two sides and the included angle	6.20

PRIMARY FRAMEWORK FOR MATHEMATICS (REVISED 2006)	POSSIBLE ERRORS
MEASURING	
Use language such as 'greater', 'smaller, 'heavier' or 'lighter' to compare quantities	6.1; 6.2; 6.3; 6.10; 6.11; 6.12
Use everyday language related to time; order and sequence familiar events and measure short periods of time with a non-standard unit	6.14
Year 1	
Estimate, measure, weigh and compare objects, choosing and using suitable uniform non-standard or standard units and measuring instruments, e.g. a lever balance, metre stick or measuring jug	6.1; 6.2; 6.3; 6.10; 6.11; 6.12
Use vocabulary related to time; order days of the week and months; read the time to the hour and half hour	6.14
Year 2	
Estimate, compare and measure lengths, masses and capacities using standard units (m, cm, kg, litre) and suitable measuring instruments	6.4; 6.5; 6.10; 6.11; 6.12
Read the numbered divisions on a scale, and interpret the divisions between them, e.g. on a scale from 0 to 25 with intervals of 1 shown but only the divisions 0, 5, 10, 15 and 20 numbered; use a ruler to draw and measure lines to the nearest centimetre	6.4
Use units of time (seconds, minutes, hours, days) and know the relationships between them; read the time to the quarter hour and identify time intervals, including those that cross the hour boundary	6.15; 6.16
Year 3	
Know the relationships between kilometres and metres, metres and centimetres, kilograms and grams, litres and millilitres; choose and use appropriate units to estimate, measure, and record measurements	6.4; 6.5
Read, to the nearest division and half-division, scales that are numbered or partially numbered; use the information to measure and draw to a suitable degree of accuracy	6.4; 6.5
Read the time on a 12-hour digital clock and to the nearest five minutes on an analogue clock; calculate time intervals and find start or end times for a given time interval	6.15; 6.16

PRIMARY FRAMEWORK FOR MATHEMATICS (REVISED 2006)	POSSIBLE ERRORS
MEASURING	
Year 4	
Use standard metric units and their abbreviations when estimating, measuring and recording length, mass and capacity; know the meaning of kilo, centi- and milli- and, where appropriate, use decimal notation to record measurements, e.g. 1.3m or 0.6kg	6.4; 6.5; 6.13
Interpret intervals and divisions on partially numbered scales and record readings accurately, where appropriate to the nearest tenth of a unit	6.4; 6.5; 6.13
Draw rectangles and measure and calculate their perimeters, find the area of rectilinear shapes drawn on a square grid by counting squares	6.6; 6.7; 6.8
Read time to the nearest minute; use a.m., p.m. and 12-hour clock notation; choose units of time to measure time intervals; calculate time intervals from clocks and timetables	6.15; 6.16
Year 5	
Read, choose, use and record standard metric units to estimate and measure length, mass and capacity to a suitable degree; convert larger to smaller units using decimals to one place, e.g. change 2.6kg to 2600g	6.4; 6.5; 6.9; 6.13
Estimate measurements of length, mass and capacity to a required degree of accuracy, e.g. the nearest centimetre; interpret a reading that lies between two unnumbered divisions on a scale	6.4; 6.5
Draw and measure lines to the nearest millimetre; measure and calculate the perimeter of regular and irregular polygons; use the formula for the area of a rectangle to calculate its area	6.6; 6.7; 6.8; 6.9
Read timetables and time using 24-hour clock notation; use a calendar to calculate time intervals	3.19

PRIMARY FRAMEWORK FOR MATHEMATICS (REVISED 2006)	POSSIBLE ERRORS
MEASURING	
Year 6	
Use standard metric units of measure and convert between units using decimals to two places notation, e.g. change 2.75 litres to 2750ml, or vice versa	6.4; 6.5; 6.9; 6.13
Read and interpret scales on a range of measuring instruments, recognising that the measurement made is approximate and recording results to a required degree of accuracy; compare readings on different scales, for example when using different instruments	6.6; 6.7; 6.8; 6.9
Calculate the perimeter and area of rectilinear shapes; estimate the area of an irregular shape by counting squares	6.6; 6.7; 6.8
Year 6 progression to Year 7	
Convert between related metric units using decimals to three places, e.g. convert 1375mm to 1.375m, or vice versa	4.3
Solve problems by measuring, estimating and calculating; measure and calculate using imperial units still in everyday use; know their approximate metric values	6.4; 6.9; 6.13

PRIMARY FRAMEWORK FOR MATHEMATICS (REVISED 2006)	POSSIBLE ERRORS
HANDLING DATA	
Foundation Stage	
Sort familiar objects to identify their similarities and differences	7.17
Count how many objects share a particular property, presenting results using pictures, drawings or numerals	7.2; 7.3; 7.4
Year 1	
Answer a question by recording information in lists and tables; present outcomes using practical resources, pictures, block graphs or pictograms	7.2; 7.3; 7.4
Use diagrams to sort objects into groups according to a given criterion; suggest a different criterion for grouping the same objects	7.15; 7.16; 7.17
Year 2	
Answer a question by recording data in lists and tables; represent the data as block graphs or pictograms to show results; use ICT to organise and present data	7.2; 7.3; 7.4
Use lists, tables and diagrams to sort objects against one or two criteria; explain choices using appropriate language, including 'not'	7.15; 7.16; 7.17; 7.18
Year 3	
Answer a question by organising, representing and interpreting data; use tally charts, frequency tables, pictograms and bar charts to highlight results and observations; use ICT to create a simple bar chart	7.2; 7.3; 7.4
Use Venn diagrams or Carroll diagrams to sort data and objects using more than one criterion	7.15; 7.16; 7.17; 7.18
Year 4	
Answer a question by identifying what data to collect; organise, present, analyse and interpret the data in tables, diagrams, tally charts, pictograms and bar charts, using ICT where appropriate	7.1; 7.2; 7.3; 7.4; 7.5

PRIMARY FRAMEWORK FOR MATHEMATICS (REVISED 2006)	POSSIBLE ERRORS
HANDLING DATA	
Year 5	
Describe the occurrence of familiar events using the language of chance or likelihood	7.25; 7.26
Answer a set of related questions by collecting, selecting and organising relevant data; draw conclusions, using ICT to present features, and identify further questions to ask	7.2; 7.3; 7.4; 7.5; 7.6; 7.7; 7.8; 7.9; 7.10
Find and interpret the mode of a set of data	7.22; 7.23
Year 6	
Describe and predict outcomes from data using the language of chance or likelihood	7.25; 7.26
Solve problems by collecting, selecting, processing, presenting and interpreting data, using ICT where appropriate; draw conclusions and identify any further questions to ask	7.2; 7.3; 7.4; 7.5; 7.6; 7.7; 7.8; 7.9; 7.10
Construct and interpret frequency tables, bar charts with grouped discrete data, and line graphs; interpret pie charts	7.5; 7.6; 7.7; 7.8; 7.9; 7.10; 7.11; 7.12; 7.13; 7.14; 7.19
Describe and interpret results and solutions to problems using the mode, range, median and mean	7.21; 7.22; 7.24
Year 6 progression to Year 7	
Understand and use the probability scale from 0 to 1; find and justify probabilities based on equally likely outcomes in simple contexts	7.25; 7.26
Analyse data from surveys and practical experiments by selecting, processing, presenting and interpreting data; plan how to collect and organise small sets of data; construct, on paper and using ICT, graphs and diagrams to represent data; compare proportions in two pie charts with different totals; identify ways of extending the survey or experiment	7.5; 7.6; 7.7; 7.8; 7.9; 7.10; 7.11; 7.12; 7.13; 7.14; 7.19
Write a short report of a statistical enquiry and illustrate with appropriate diagrams, graphs and charts, using ICT as appropriate; justify the choice of what is presented	7.5; 7.6; 7.7; 7.8; 7.9; 7.10; 7.11; 7.12; 7.13; 7.14; 7.19

References

Ackermann, E. (1991) From decontextualized to situated knowledge: revisiting Piaget's water-level experiment, in I. Harel and S. Papert (eds) *Constructionism*. Norwood, NJ: Ablex Publishing Corporation.

Ainley, J., Bagnib, G.T., Hefendehl–Hebekerc, L., Lagranged, J.B. (2009) Algebraic thinking and mathematics education. In: *Proceedings of CERME* 6, January 28th February 1st 2009, Lyon, France 2010 pp. 415–419.

Ainley, J., Bills, L., Wilson, K.E. (2005) Designing Spreadsheet-based Tasks for Purposeful Algebra, *International Journal of Computers for Mathematical Learning*, Vol. 10(3). pp. 191–215.

Ainley, J., Nardi, E. and Pratt, D. (2000) 'Towards the Construction of Meanings for Trend in Active Graphing', *International Journal of Computers for Mathematical Learning* 5(2), 85–114.

Ainley J., Pratt, D and Hansen, A. (2006) Connecting Engagement and Focus in Pedagogic Task Design. *British Educational Research Journal*, 32(1): 23–38.

Anghileri, J. (ed.) (1995) *Children's Mathematical Thinking in the Primary Years: Perspectives on Children's Learning*. London: Cassell.

Anghileri, J. (2000) *Teaching Number Sense*. London: Continuum.

Anghilieri, J. and Baron, S. (1999) Playing with the materials of study: poleidoblocs, *Education 3–13*, 27(2): 57–64.

Askew, M. and Wiliam, D. (1995) *Recent Research in Mathematics Education 5–16*. London: HMSO.

Askew, M., Brown, M., Rhodes,V., Johnson, D. and Wiliam, D. (1997) *Effective Teachers of Numeracy. Final Report*. London: King's College.

Atiyah, M. (2001) Mathematics in the 20th century: geometry versus algebra. *Mathematics Today*, 37(2): 47–9.

Bailey, D.H. and Borwein, J.M. (2010) The greatest mathematical discovery? Available from http://www.fas.org/sgp/eprint/discovery.pdf. Last accessed 7/9/10.

Baroody, A.J., Lai, M. and Mix, K.S. (2006) The development of young children's early number and operation sense and its implications for early childhood education. In B. Spodek and O. N. Saracho (Eds.) *Handbook of research on the education of the young*. 2nd Ed. Mahwah, NJ: Lawrence Erlbaum Associates. pp. 187–222.

Barr, R. (2010) Transfer of learning between 2D and 3D sources during infancy: Informing theory and practice. *Developmental Review* Volume 30, Issue 2, pp 128–154.

Barret, J.E. and Clements, D.H. (2003) Quantifying Path Length: Fourth-Grade Children's Developing Abstractions for Linear Measurement. *Cognition and instruction*, 21(4): 475–520.

Battista, M.T. (1990) Spacial visualisation and gender differences in high school geometry. *Journal for Research in Mathematics Education*, 21: 47–60.

BECTa (1998) *Using IT to support English, Maths and Science at KS2*. BECTa.

Bell, A., Swan, M., Onslow, B., Pratt, K. and Purdy, D. (1985) *Diagnostic teaching for long term learning: Report of ESRC Project HR8491/1*. Nottingham: Shell Centre for Mathematical Education, University of Nottingham.

Bell, A.W. (1993) Some experiments in diagnostic teaching. *Education Studies in Mathematics*, 24(1): 115–37.

Boaler, J. (2009) *The elephant in the classroom. Helping children learn and love mathematics.* London: Souvenir Press Ltd.

Booth, D. (1981) Aspects of logico-mathematical intuition in the development of young children's spontaneous pattern painting. Unpublished PhD thesis, La Trobe University.

Bouck, E.C. and Flanagan, S. M. (2009) Virtual Manipulatives: What They Are and How Teachers Can Use Them. *Intervention in School and Clinic*. Sage Publications. Available from http://isc.sagepub.com/content/early/2009/11/04/1053451209349530.full.pdf. Last accessed 9/9/10.

Brannon, E. M., Lutz, D. and Cordes S. (2006) The development of area discrimination and its implications for number representation in infancy. *Development Science*; 9(6): F59–F64.

Brown, M. (1981) Number operations, in K.M. Hart (ed.) *Children's Understanding of Mathematics 11–16*. London: John Murray.

Briggs, M. and Pritchard, A. (2002). *Using ICT in Primary Mathematics Teaching*. Exeter:Learning Matters.

Brueckner, L.J. (1928) Analysis of Errors in Fractions *The Elementary School Journal* Vol. 28, No. 10. pp. 760–770.

Bruner, J. (1960) *The Process of Education*. 1st edition. Cambridge, MA: Harvard University Press.

Bruner, J. (1977) *The Process of Education*. 2nd edition. Cambridge, MA: Harvard University Press.

Bryant, P. (1982) The role of conflict and agreement between intellectual strategies in children's ideas about measurement, *British Journal of Psychology*. 73: 243–52.

Burger, M. and Shaugnessy, J.M. (1986) Characterizing the van Hiele levels of development in geometry. *Journal for Research in Mathematics Education*, 17: 31–4.

Burton, L. (1990) *Gender and Mathematics: An International Perspective*. London: Cassell.

Carpenter, T., Fennema, E. and Romberg, T. (1993) *Rational Numbers: an Integration of Research*. Hillsdale, NJ: Lawrence Erlbaum Associates.

Carpenter, T.P. and Moser, J.M. (1979) The development of addition and subtraction concepts in young children, in *Proceedings of the Third International Conference for the Psychology of Mathematics Education*. University of Warwick, Mathematics Education Research Centre.

Carpenter, T.P. and Moser, J.M. (1982) The development of addition and subtraction problem solving skill, in *Addition and Subtraction: A Cognitive Perspective*, Carpenter *et al.*, (eds). Hillsdale, NJ: Lawrence Erlbaum.

Casey, R. (2002) A framework for teaching mathematically promising pupils. In V. Koshy and J. Murray (Eds) *Unlocking Numeracy*. London: David Fulton. pp. 122–145.

Castle, K. and Needham, J. (2007) First graders' understanding of measurement. *Early Childhood Education Journal* Volume 35, Number 3, 215-221.

Charalambous, C.Y. and Pitta-Pantazi, D. (2005) Revisiting a theoretical model on fractions: Implications for teaching and research. In Chick, H. L. and Vincent, J. L. (Eds.). *Proceedings of the 29th Conference of the International Group for the Psychology of Mathematics Education*, Vol. 2, pp. 233–240. Melbourne: PME. Available from http://www.emis.de/proceedings/PME29/ PME29RRPapers/PME29Vol2CharalambousEtAl.pdf Last accessed 7/9/10.

References

Circa (1997) Pictures from data. *Circa: The Mathematical Magazine.* Volume 6.

Clements, D.H. (2003) Major themes and recommendations, in D.H. Clements, J. Sarama and A.M. DiBiase *Engaging Young Children in Mathematics: Standards for Early Childhood Mathematics Education.* London: Routledge. pp 7–72.

Clements, D.H. and Battista, M.T. (1990a) Constructivist learning and teaching, *Arithmetic Teacher.* 38(1): 34–5.

Clements, D.H. and Battista, M.T. (1990b) The effects of Logo on children's conceptualisations of angle and polygons, *Journal for Research in Mathematics Education,* 21: 356–71.

Clements, D.H. and Battista, M.T. (1992) Geometry and spatial reasoning, in D.A. Grouws (ed.) *Handbook of Research in Mathematics Teaching and Learning.* New York: Macmillan Publishing Company, pp. 420–64.

Clements, D.D., Battista, M.T., Sarama, J. and Swaminathan, S. (1996) Development of turn and turn measurement concepts in a computer-based instructional unit, *Educational Studies in Mathematics,* 18: 109–24.

Clements, D.D. and Burns, B.A (2005) Students' development of strategies for turn and angle measure. *Educational Studies in Mathematics* Volume 41, Number 1, 31–45.

Clements, D.D., Sarama, J. and Swaminathan, S. (1997) Young children's concepts of shape, *Proceedings for International Group for Mathematics Education,* 21: 356–71.

Clements, D.H. and Sarama, J. (2009) *Learning and Teaching Early Math: The Learning Trajectories Approach.* London: Routledge.

Clements, M.A. (1980) Analyzing children's errors on written mathematical tasks, *Educational Studies in Mathematics,* 11(1): 1–21.

Cobb, P. (1987) Information-processing psychology and mathematics education – a constructivist perspective, *Journal of Mathematical Behaviour,* 6: 3–40.

Cobb, P., Yackel, E. and Wood, T. (1989) Young children's emotional acts while doing mathematical problem solving, in D.B. McLeod and V.M. Adams (eds) *Affect and Mathematical Problem Solving: A New Perspective,* New York: Springer-Verlag, pp. 117–48.

Cockburn, A. (1999) *Teaching mathematics with insight.* London: Falmer Press.

Cockcroft, W.H. (1982) *Mathematics Counts.* London: HMSO.

Cole, R. (2009) Why today's children don't understand money: A cashless society has left today's children with no understanding of the value of real money — let alone where it actually comes from. *The Times.* August 1st 2009.

Collins, A., Brown, J.S. and Newton, S.E. (1990) Cognitive apprenticeship: teaching the crafts of reading, writing and mathematics, in L.B. Resnick (ed.) *Knowing, Learning and Instruction: Essays in Honor of Robert Glaser.* Hillsdale, NJ: Lawrence Erlbaum.

Cross, C.T., Woods, T.A and Schweingruber, H. (2009) *Mathematics Learning in Early Childhood: Paths Toward Excellence and Equity.* Washington, D.C: The National Academies Press.

Critchley, P. (2002) Chocolate fractions. *Times Educational Supplement,* 19 January.

Carruthers, E. and Worthington, M. (2006) *Children's Mathematics: Making Marks, Making Meaning.* 2nd Ed. London: SAGE Publications.

Dauben, J.W. and Scriba, C. J. (Eds.) (2002) *Writing the history of mathematics: Its historical development.* Berlin: Birkhäuser Verlag.

Davis, R.B. (1986) Conceptual and procedural knowledge in mathematics: a summary analysis, in J. Heibert (ed.) *Conceptual and Procedural Knowledge: The Case of Mathematics.* Hillsdale, NJ: Lawrence Erlbaum Associates, pp. 265–300.

Deboys, M. and Pitt, E. (1988) *Lines of Development in Primary Mathematics.* 3rd edition. Belfast: The Blackstaff Press.

de Court, E., Greer, B. and Verschaffel, L. (2000) *Making sense of word problems* London: Taylor & Francis.

Department for Education (2010) Developing Mathematics in Initial Teacher Training. (Webpage url unavailable at time of writing).

Department for Education and Employment (1998a) *Teaching: High Status, High Standards. Requirements for Courses of Initial Teacher Training. Circular 4/98.* London: DfEE.

Department for Education and Employment (1999a) *Mathematics. The National Curriculum for England: Key Stages 1–4.* London: DfEE Publications.

Department for Education and Employment (1999b) *Framework for Teaching Mathematics from Reception to Year 6.* London: DfEE Publications.

Department for Education and Employment (1999c) *Professional Development Materials 3 and 4: Guide for your Professional Development, Book 2: Raising Standards in Mathematics at Key Stage 2.* London: DfEE.

Department for Education and Employment (1999d) *Professional Development Materials 3 and 4: Guide for your Professional Development, Book 3: Raising Standards in Mathematics at Key Stage 2.* London: DfEE.

Department for Education and Employment (1994) *Mathematical Vocabulary.* London: DfEE.

Department for Education and Employment (2000) *Curriculum Guidance for the Foundation Stage.* London: QCA.

Department for Education and Employment (2002a) *Qualifying to Teach Professional Standards for Qualified Teacher Status and Requirements for Initial Teacher Training.* London: Teacher Training Agency.

Department for Education and Employment (2002b) Mathematics unit plans. www.standards.dfes.gov.uk/numeracy/unit_plans/ Accessed 21 March 2005.

Department for Education and Employment/Qualifications and Curriculum Authority (1998) *Science: A Scheme of Work for Key Stages 1 and 2.* London: DfEE.

Department for Education and Employment (2005) *The Early Years Foundation Stage Statutory Framework: Setting the standards for learning, development and care for children from birth to five.* London: DfEE Publications. Ref00013-2007BKT-EN.

Department for Education and Skills (2003) *Models and Images: Y1–Y3.* London: DfES Publications. Ref. 0508–2003 GCDI.

Department for Education and Skills (2004) *Primary National Strategy. Excellence and Enjoyment: Learning and Teaching in the Primary Years. Creating a Learning Culture. Conditions for Learning.* London: DfES Publications. Ref. 0523–2004.

Department for Education and Skills (2005) *Primary National Strategy. Targeting Support: Implementing Interventions for Children with Significant Difficulties in Mathematics.* London: DfES Publications. Ref. 1083–2005.

DfES (2008) Independent review of mathematics teaching in early years settings and primary schools. Final report. Ref. 00433-2008BKT-EN. Available from http://publications.education.gov.uk/eOrderingDownload/WMR%20Final%20Report.pdf. Last accessed 1/12/10.

Dewey, J. (1926) *Democracy and Education: An Introduction to the Philosophy of Education.* New York: The Macmillan Company.

Dickson, L., Brown, M. and Gibson, O. (1984) *Children Learning Mathematics: A Teacher's Guide to Recent Research.* London: Cassell Education.

DiSessa, A. and Sherin, B. (1998) What changes in conceptual change? *International Science Education,* 20(10): 1155–91.

Donaldson, M. (1978) *Children's Minds.* London: Fontana Press.

Donlan, C. (2003) Numeracy development in children with specific language impairments: The interaction of conceptual and procedural knowledge. In A. J. Baroody and A. Dowker (Eds.) *The development of arithmetic concepts and skills: Constructing adaptive expertise.* Mahwah, NJ: Erlbaum. Pp. 337-358.

Driscoll, M.P. (1994) *Psychology of Learning for Instruction.* Needham, MA: Allyn and Bacon.

Duncan, A. (1996) *What Primary Teachers Should Know about MATHS.* London: Hodder and Stoughton.

Elwood, J. and Gipps, C. (1998) *Review of Recent Research on the Achievement of Girls in Single Sex Schools.* London: Institute of Education: University of London.

English, L. (2002) Development of 10-year-olds' mathematical modelling, in A.D. Cockburn and E. Nardi (eds) *Proceedings of the Twenty-sixth Annual Conference of the International Group for the Psychology of Mathematics Education Conference,* 3: 329–35.

Fischbein, E. (1993). The theory of figural concepts, *Educational Studies in Mathematics,* 24: 139–62.

Fischbein, E. (1994) The interaction between the formal, the algorithmic and the intuitive components in a mathematical activity. In R. Biehler *et al.* (eds) *Didactics of Mathematics as a Scientific Discipline.* Dordrecht: Reidel.

Fisher, I. (2001). Maths resource introducing probability. *Mathematics in School,* 30(3).

Flegg, G. (ed.) (1989) *Number Through the Ages.* London and Milton Keynes: Macmillan Education in association with the Open University.

Foster, R. (1994) Counting on success in simple addition tasks. *Proceedings of the 18th Conference of the International Group for the Psychology of Mathematics Education,* 2: 360–7.

Foster, R. (1996) Practice makes imperfect. *Mathematics Teaching,* 143 (June): 34–6.

Freudenthal, H. (1971) Geometry between the devil and the deep sea, *Educational Studies in Mathematics,* 3: 413–35.

Freudenthal, H. (1973) *Mathematics as an Educational Task.* Dordrecht: Reidel.

Freudenthal, H. (1981) Major problems of mathematical education, *Educational Studies in Mathematics,* 12: 133–50.

Freudenthal, H. (1991) *Revisiting Mathematics Education.* Dordrecht: Kluwer Academic Publishers.

Frobisher, L., Monaghan, J., Orton, A., Roper, T. and Threlfall, J. (1999) *Learning to Teach Number.* Cheltenham: Stanley Thornes.

Fujita, T. and Jones, K. (2002) The design of geometry teaching: learning from the geometry textbooks of Godfrey and Siddons, in O. McNamara (ed.) *Proceedings of the Twenty-third Day Conference of the British Society for Research into Learning Mathematics.* London: British Society of Research into Learning Mathematics.

Fuson, K.C. (1992) Research on whole number addition and subtraction, in D.A. Grows (ed.) *Handbook of Research on Mathematics Teaching and Learning.* New York: Macmillan.

Fuys, D., Geddes, D. and Tischler, R. (1988) The van Hiele model of thinking in geometry among adolescents, *Journal for Research in Mathematics Education Monograph.* 3.

Garrick, R. (2002) Pattern-making and pattern play in the nursery: special organisation. Paper presented at the *Annual Conference of the British Educational Research Association,* University of Exeter, England, 12–14 September.

Garrick, R., Threlfall, J. and Orton, A. (2004) Pattern in the nursery. In A. Orton *Patterns in teaching and learning of maths.* London: Continuum pp. 1–17.

Geary, D.C. (1996) Sexual selection and sex differences in mathematical abilities, *Behavioural and Brain Sciences,* 19: 224–47.

Gelman, R. and Gallistel, C.R. (1986*) The Child's Understanding of Number.* London:Harvard University Press.

Gelman, R. and Gallistel, C.R. (2004) Language and the origin of numerical concepts. *Science,* 306(5695): 441–443.

Gibson, O.E. (1981) A study of the ability of children with spina bifida to handle money. PhD thesis, University of London.

Ginsburg, H.P. (1977) *Children's Arithmetic: How They Learn It and How You Teach It.* Austin, TX: PRO-ED.

Glasersfled von, E. (1995) *Radical Constructivism: A Way of Knowing and Learning.* London: RoutledgeFalmer.

Goulding, M. (2002) Primary teacher trainees' self-assessment of their mathematical subject knowledge. Paper presented at the Annual Conference of the British Educational Research Association, University of Exeter, England, 12–14 September.

Graham, A. (1990) *Supporting Primary Mathematics: Probability.* Prepared by the supporting primary mathematics. Milton Keynes: Centre for Mathematics Education, Open University.

Gravemeijer, K. and Doorman, M. (1999) Context problems in realistic mathematics education: a calculus course as an example, *Educational Studies in Mathematics,* 39: 111–29.

Gray, E. (2008) Compressing the counting process: strength from the flexible interpretation of symbols. In Thompson, I. (ed.) (2008) *Teaching and Learning Early Number.* 2nd Ed. Buckingham: Open University Press. pp. 82–94.

Gray, E.M. and Tall, D. (1994) Duality, ambiguity and flexibility: a proceptual view of simple arithmetic, *Journal for Research in Mathematics Education,* 26: 115–41.

Greeno, J.G. (1980) Some examples of cognitive task analysis with instructional implications, in R.E. Snow, P. Frederico and W.E. Montague (eds) *Aptitude, Learning and Instruction, Vol. 2: Cognitive Process Analysis of Learning and Problem-Solving.* Hillsdale, NJ: Lawrence Erlbaum Associates, pp. 1–21.

Guitierréz, A., Jaime, A. and Fortuny, J.M. (1991) An alternative paradigm to evaluate the van Hiele levels, *Journal for Research into Mathematics Education,* 3: 17–24.

Hall, E. (2007) Mixed messages: *The role and value of drawing in early education*. Paper presented at the British Educational Research Association Annual Conference, Institute of Education, University of London. 5-8 September, 2007. Available from http://www.leeds.ac.uk/educol/documents/165704.htm. Last accessed 10/9/10.

Hall, J. S. (2000) Psychology and schooling: the impact of Susan Isaacs and Jean Piaget on 1960s science education reform. *History of Education*, Vol. 29, Issue 2. pp. 153 – 170.

Harel, I. and Papert, S. (1991) *Constructionism*. Norwood, NJ: Ablex Publishing Corporation.

Hasegawa, J. (1997) Concept formation of triangles and quadrilaterals in second grade, *Educational Studies in Mathematics*, 32: 157–79.

Hatch, G. (1998) Replace your mental arithmetic test with a game, *Mathematics in School*, 27(1): 32–5.

Haylock, D. (2001) *Mathematics Explained for Primary Teachers*. 2nd edition. London: Paul Chapman Publishing.

Haylock, D. and Cockburn, A. (1997) *Understanding Mathematics in the Lower Primary Years*. London: Paul Chapman Publishing.

Hausfather, S.J. (1996) Vygotsky and schooling: creating a social context for learning. *Action in Education*, 18: 1–10.

Hershkowitz, R. (1990) Psychological aspects of learning geometry, in P. Nesher and J. Kilpatrick (eds) *Mathematics and Cognition*. Cambridge: Cambridge University Press, pp. 70–95.

Hershkowitz, R., Ben-Chaim, D., Hoyles, C., Lappan, G., Mitchelmore, M. and Vinner, S. (1990) Psychological aspects of learning geometry, in P. Nesher and J. Kilpatrick (eds) *Mathematics and Cognition: A Research Synthesis by the International Group for the Psychology of Mathematics Education*. Cambridge: Cambridge Universtiy Press, pp. 70–95.

Hilbert, D. and Cohn-Vossen, S. (1932) *Geometry and the Imagination*. New York: Chelsea.

Hill, P.S. (1908) The Value and Limitations of Froebel's Gifts as Educative Materials Parts I, II *The Elementary School Teacher*, Vol. 9, No. 3. pp. 129-137.

Hopkins, C., Gifford, S. and Pepperell, S. (1999) *Mathematics in the Primary School: A Sense of Progression*. 2nd edition. London: David Fulton Publishers.

Hopkins, C., Pope, S. and Pepperell, S. (2004) *Understanding Primary Mathematics*. London: David Fulton Publishers.

Hoyles, C. (1985) What is the point of group discussion in mathematics? *Educational Studies in Mathematics*, 16: 205–14.

Hoyles, C. and Sutherland, R. (1986) *When 45 Equals 60*. London: University of London Institute of Education, Microworlds Project.

Huckstep, P., Rowland, T. and Thwaites, A. (2002) Primary teachers' mathematics content knowledge: what does it look like in the classroom? Paper presented at the *Annual Conference of the British Educational Research Association*, University of Exeter, England, 12–14 September.

Hughes, M. (1986) *Children and Number: Difficulties in Learning Mathematics*. Oxford: Blackwell.

Hughes, M. and Vass, A. (2001) *Strategies for Closing the Learning Gap*. Stafford: Network Educational Press.

Johnson, S. (1996) The contribution of large scale assessment programmes to research on gender differences *Educational Research and Evaluation*, 2.1: 25–49.

Jones, K. (2000) Providing a foundation for deductive reasoning: Students' interpretations when using dynamic geometry software and their evolving mathematical explanations, *Educational Studies in Mathematics*, 44: 55–85.

Jones, K. (2003) Classroom implications of research on dynamic geometry software. Paper presented to the Thematic Working Group: Tools and technologies in mathematical didactics, CERME 3: Third Conference of the European Society for Research in Mathematics Education 28 February-3 March 2003 in Bellaria, Italy.

Kafai, Y. and Harel, I. (1991a) Learning through design and teaching: exploring social and collaborative aspects of constructionism, in I. Harel and S. Papert (eds) *Constructionism*. Norwood, NJ: Ablex.

Kafai, Y. and Harel, I. (1991b) Learning through consulting: when mathematical ideas, knowledge of programming and design, and playful discourse are intertwined, in I. Harel and S. Papert (eds) *Constructionism*. Norwood, NJ: Ablex.

Karmarkar, U.R. and Buonomano, D.V. (2007) Telling time in the absence of clocks. *Neuron*. Vol. 53(3): 427–438.

Kazemi, E. (1998) Discourse that promotes conceptual understanding, *Teaching Children Mathematics Journal*, March: 410–14.

Keat, J. B. and Wilburne, J.M. (2009) The impact of storybooks on kindergarten children's mathematical achievement and approaches to learning. *US-China Education Review*. Vol. 6, No.7. pp. 61-67.

Kelly, C.A. (2006) Using manipulatives in mathematical problem solving: a performance-based analysis. *The Montana Mathematics Enthusiast (TMME)*, vol3, no.2, pp.184-193. Available from http://www.math.umt.edu/tmme/vol3no2/tmmevol3no2_colorado_pp184_193. pdf Last accessed 10/9/10.

Koedinger, K.R. and Nathan, M.J. (2004) The Real Story Behind Story Problems: Effects of Representations on Quantitative Reasoning *Journal of the Learning Sciences*, Vol. 13(2) pp. 129–164.

Koshy, V. (2000) Children's mistakes and misconceptions, in V. Koshy, P. Ernest and R.Casey (eds) *Mathematics for Primary Teachers*. London: Routledge.

Lamberg, T. and Middleton, J. (2002) The role of inscriptional practices in the development of mathematical ideas in a fifth grade classroom, in A.D. Cockburn and E. Nardi (eds) *Proceedings of the Twenty-sixth Annual Conference of the International Group for the Psychology of Mathematics Education Conference*. Norwich: University of East Anglia.

Lamon, S.L. (2001) Presenting and representing: From fractions to rational numbers. In A. Cuoco and F. Curcio (eds.), *The roles of representation in school mathematics-2001 Yearbook*. Reston: NCTM. pp. 146–165.

Lamon, S.L. (2008) Teaching Fractions and Ratios for Understanding: Essential Content Knowledge and Instructional Strategies for Teachers. 2nd Ed. Mahwah, NJ: Lawrence Erlbaum Associates.

Lave, J. (1988) *Cognition in Practice: Mind, Mathematics and Culture in Everyday Life*. Cambridge: Cambridge University Press.

References

Lave, J. and Wenger, E. (1991) *Situated Learning: Legitimate Peripheral Participation*. Cambridge: Cambridge University Press.

Liebeck, P. (1984) *How Children Learn Mathematics*. London: Penguin Books.

Moloney, K. and Stacey, K. (1997) Changes with Age in Students' Conceptions of Decimal Notation. *Mathematics Education Research Journal*. Vol. 9, No.1, 25–38.

Masingila, J.O. (1993) Connecting the ethnomath of carpet layers with school learning. *International Study Group on Ethnomathematics (ISGEm) Newsletter*, 8:2.

Mathematics Association (1987) *Maths Talk*. Cheltenham: Stanley Thornes.

Matthews, J. (1999) *The Art of Childhood and Adolescence: The Construction of Meaning*. London: Falmer Press.

Misailidou, C., and Williams, J. (2002). Ratio: Raising Teachers' Awareness of Children's Thinking. *Proceedings of the 2nd International Conference on the teaching of Mathematics at the undergraduate level* (ICTM2). Available from: http://www.math.uoc.gr/~ictm2/Proceedings/pap143.pdf Last accessed 9/9/10.

Mitchelmore, M.C. and White, P. (2000) Development of angle concepts by progressive abstraction and generalisation. *Educational Studies in Mathematics* 41: 209–238.

Monaghan, F. (2000). What difference does it make? Children's views of the difference between some quadrilaterals. *Educational Studies in Mathematics*, 42: 179–96.

Monroe, E. and Clark, H. (1998) Rote or reason, *Mathematics in School*, 27(3): 26–7.

Mooney, C., Ferrie, L., Fox, S., Hansen, A. and Wrathmell, R. (2002) *Achieving QTS. Primary Mathematics: Knowledge and Understanding*. 2nd edition. Exeter: Learning Matters.

Morton, R.L. (1924) An Analysis of Pupils' Errors in Fractions. *The Journal of Educational Research* Vol. 9, No. 2 pp. 117–125.

Mulligan, J., Prescott, A., Mitchelmore, M. (2004) Children's development of structure in early mathematics. In Watson, J. and Beswick, K. (eds.) Proceedings of the 30th annual conference of the Mathematics Education Research Group of Australasia (MERGA). Available from http://www.erikson.edu/earlymath/content/MulliganPME2004.pdf. Last accessed 10/9/10.

Munn, P. (2008) Children's beliefs about counting. In Thompson, I. (ed.) *Teaching and Learning Early Number* (2nd ed). Buckingham: Open University Press. pp 19–33.

National Institute for Budget Advice (2009) Learning to manage money: NIBUD learning goals and competences for children and young people. Utrecht: NIBUD. Available from http://www.nibud.nl/fileadmin/user_upload/Documenten/PDF/nibud_learning_goals_and_competences.pdf. Last accessed 7/9/10.

NCTM (2000) Data analysis and probability standard for grades 6–8. Available from: www.orangeusd.k12.ca.us/vorba/statistics.htm Accessed 6 March 2005.

Newman, M.A. (1977) An analysis of sixth-grade pupils' errors in written mathematical tasks in M. Clements and J. Foyster (eds.) *Research in Mathematics Education in Australia*, 2: 269–287.

Nickson, M. (2000) *Teaching and Learning Mathematics: A Teachers Guide to Recent Research and its Application*. London: Cassell.

Noss, R. and Hoyles, C. (1996) *Windows on Mathematical Meanings: Learning Cultures and Computers*. Dordrecht: Kluwer Academic Publishers.

Nunes, T. and Bryant, P. (1996) *Children Doing Mathematics*. Oxford: Blackwell Publishers.

Nunes, T., Bryant, P., Evans, D., Bell, D., Gardner, S. Gardner, A. and Carraher, J. (2007) The contribution of logical reasoning to the learning of mathematics in primary school. *British Journal of Developmental Psychology*, Volume 25, Number 1, March 2007 , pp. 147–166(20).

Nunes, T., Schliemann, A.D. and Carraher, D.W. (1993) *Street Mathematics and School Mathematics*. Cambridge: Cambridge University Press.

Nyabanyaba, T. (1999) Wither relevance? Mathematics teachers' discussion of the use of 'real-life' contexts in school mathematics, in *For the Learning of Mathematics*, 19(3): 10–14.

OFSTED (2003) *The National Literacy and Numeracy Strategies and the Primary Curriculum*. London: HMI.

Ollerton, M. (2000) Learning mathematics through 'real-life' problems: texts, contexts and con-tricks, *Mathematics Teaching* 166: 12.

Orton, A. (1992) *Learning Mathematics Issues, Theory and Classroom Practice*. 2nd edition. London: Cassell.

Orton, A. and Frobisher, L. (2005) *Insights into Teaching Mathematics*. 2nd edition. London: Continuum.

Orton, J. (1997) Pupils' perception of pattern in relation to shape. *Proceedings of the 21st Conference of the International Group for the Psychology of Mathematics Education*, 3: 304–11.

Orton, J. (2004) Children's perception of pattern in relation to shape. In A. Orton *Patterns in teaching and learning of maths*. London: Continuum pp149–167.

Pagni, D. (2004). Fractions and decimals. *Australian Mathematics Teacher*. Vol. 60(4), pp. 28–30.

Pegg, J. and Tall, D. (2002) Fundamental cycles of cognitive growth, in A. D. Cockburn and E. Nardi (eds) *Proceedings of the Twenty-sixth Annual Conference of the International Group for the Psychology of Mathematics Education Conference*, 4: 41–8.

Personal Finance Education Group (2010) Financial capability in England. Available from http://www.pfeg.org/curriculum_and_policy/england/index.html. Last accessed 7/9/10.

Piaget, J. (1953) *How Children Form Mathematical Concepts*. San Francisco: W.H. Freeman and Co. (reprinted from *Scientific American*, November 1953).

Piaget, J. (1970) *The Science of Education and the Psychology of the Child*. New York: Crossman.

Piaget, J. (1971) *The Psychology of Intelligence*. London: Routledge and Kegan Paul.

Piaget, J. and Inhelder, B. (1969) *The Psychology of the Child*. London: Routledge and Kegan Paul.

Piaget, J., Inhelder, B. and Szeminska, A. (1970) *The child's conception of geometry*. London: Routledge

Picard, D. and Durand, K. (2004) Are young children's drawings canonically based? *Journal of Experimental Child Psychology* Volume 90, Issue 1, Pages 48-64.

Pound, L. (1999) *Supporting Mathematical Development in the Early Years*. Buckingham: Open University Press.

Pratt, D. and Noss, R. (2002) The micro-evolution of mathematical knowledge: the case of randomness. *Journal of Learning Sciences*, 11(4): 453–88.

Qualifications and Curriculum Authority (1999) *The National Numeracy Strategy: Teaching Written Calculations, Guidance for Teachers at Key Stages 1 and 2*. London: QCA.

Qualifications and Curriculum Authority (2001) *Using Assessment to Raise Achievement in Mathematics. Key Stages 1, 2 and 3*. Research report, November 2001. London: QCA.

Rawson, B. (1993) Searching for pattern, *Education 3–13*, 21(3): 26–33.

Rees, R. and Barr, G. (1984) *Diagnostics and Prescription in the Classroom: Some Common Maths Problems*. London: Harper and Row.

Ring, K. (2001) Young children drawing: the significance of the context. Paper presented at *The British Educational Research Association Annual Conference*. University of Leeds, 13–15 September.

Rocke, J. (1995) A common cents approach to fractions, *Teaching Children Mathematics*, 2(4): 234–6.

Ryan, J. and Williams, J. (2007) *Children's Mathematics 4-15: Learning from Errors and Misconceptions*. Berkshire: Open University Press.

Saads, S. and Davis, G. (1997) Spacial abilities, van Hiele levels and language used in three dimensional geometry. *Proceedings of the 22nd Conference of the International Group for the Psychology of Mathematics Education*, 4: 104–11.

Sadi, A. (2007) Misconceptions in Numbers *UGRU Journal* Volume 5. Available from http://www.ugru.uaeu.ac.ae/UGRUJournal/UGRUJournal_files/SR5/MIN.pdf. Last accessed 9/9/10.

Sáiz, M. (2003) Primary teachers' conceptions about the concept of volume: The case of volume-measurable objects. In N.A. Pateman, B.J. Dougherty and J.T. Zilliox (eds.) *Proceedings of the 27th Psychology of Mathematics Education International Conference*. Vol. 4. pp 95–102.

Sáiz, M. and Figueras, O. (2009) A research-based workshop design for volume tasks. In B. Clarke, B. Grevholm and R. Millman (Eds.) *Tasks in primary mathematics teacher education: Purpose, use and exemplars*. New York: Springer. pp. 147–160.

Sfard, A. (1991) On the dual nature of mathematical conceptions: reflections on processes and objects as different sides of the same coin, *Educational Studies in Mathematics*, 22: 1–36.

Shuard, H. and Rothery, A. (eds) (1984) *Children Reading Mathematics*. London: John Murray.

Skemp, R. (1977) Relational understanding and instrumental understanding, *Arithmetic Teacher*, 77: 20–6.

Skemp, R.R. (1986) *The Psychology of Learning Mathematics*. 2nd edition. London: Penguin Books.

Smeets, E. and T. Mooij (2001) Pupil-centred learning, ICT, and teacher behaviour: observations in educational practice, *British Journal of Educational Technology*, 32: 403–17.

Smedslund, J. (1961) The acquisition of conservation of substance and weight in children. Scandinavian Journal of Psychology. 2: 11–20.

Smith, C. (1999) Pencil and paper numeracy, *Mathematics in School*, (2) 8(5): 10–13.

Sotto, E. (1994) *When Teaching Becomes Learning: A Theory and Practice of Teaching*. London: Continuum.

Spooner, M. (2002) *Errors and Misconceptions in Maths at Key Stage 2: Working Towards Successful SATS*. London: David Fulton Publishers.

Star, S.L. (1989) The structure of ill-structured solutions: boundary objects and heterogeneous distributed problem solving, in L. Glasser and M.N. Huhns (eds) *Distributed Intelligence*, 2: 37–54.

Steffe, L.P., Thompson, P.W. and Richards, J. (1982) Children counting in arithmetic problem solving, in *Addition and Subtraction: A Cognitive Perspective*. Hillsdale NJ: Lawrence Erlbaum.

Swan (2001) Dealing with misconceptions in mathematics, in P. Gates (ed) *Issues in Mathematics Teaching*. London: Routledge Falmer, pp. 147–65.

Swan (2003) Making sense of mathematics, in I. Thompson (ed) *Enhancing Primary Mathematics Teaching*. Berkshire: Open University Press, pp. 112–24.

Tanner, H. and Jones, S. (2000) *Becoming a Successful Teacher of Mathematics*. London: RoutledgeFalmer, pp. 86–107.

Tartre, L.A. (1990) Spatial orientation skill and mathematical problem solving. *Journal for Research in Mathematics Education*, 21: 216–29.

Teacher Training Agency (2003) *Qualifying to Teach. Handbook of Guidance*. Teacher Training Agency.

Thompson, I. (ed.) (1997) *Teaching and Learning Early Number*. Buckingham: Open University Press.

Thompson, I. (ed.) (2008) *Teaching and Learning Early Number*. 2nd Ed. Buckingham: Open University Press.

Treffers, A. (1987) *Three Dimensions. A Model of Goal and Theory Description in Mathematics Instruction: The Wiskobas Project*. Dordrecht: Reidel Publishing Company.

Twidle, J. (2006) Is the concept of conservation of volume in solids really more difficult than for liquids, or is the way we test giving us an unfair comparison? *Educational Research* Vol. 48 (1). pp 93–109.

van den Heuvel-Panhuizen (2003) The didactical use of models in realistic mathematics education: An example from a longitudinal trajectory on percentage. *Educational Studies in Mathematics*. Vol. 54(1), 9–35.

Van Hiele, P.M. (1986). *Structure and Insight: A Theory of Mathematics Education*. London: Academic Press.

Vergnaud, G. and Durand, C. (1976) Structures additives et complexite psychogenetique, *La Revue Francaise de Pedagogie*, 36: 28–43.

Vygotsky, L.S. (1978) *Mind in Society: The Development of Higher Pyschological Processes*. Cambridge, MA: Harvard University Press.

Walcott, C., Mohr, D. and Kastberg, S.E. (2009) Making sense of shape: An analysis of children's written responses. *The Journal of Mathematical Behavior*. Vol 28, Issue 1, pp. 30–40.

Warren, E. (2005) Young children's ability to generalise the pattern rule for growing patterns. In Chick, H. L. and Vincent, J. L. (eds.). *Proceedings of the 29th Conference of the International Group for the Psychology of Mathematics Education*, Vol. 4, pp. 305–312. Melbourne: PME.

Watson, A. and Mason, J. (1998) *Questions and Prompts for Mathematical Thinking*. Derby: Association of Teachers of Mathematics.

Watson, D. (ed.) (1993) *The Impact Report. An Evaluation of the Impact of Information Technology on Children's Achievements in Primary and Secondary Schools*. London: Kings College University Press.

White, P., Wilson, S., Faragher, R. and Mitchelmore, M. (2007) Percentages as Part Whole Relationships. In Watson, J. and Beswick, K. (eds.) Proceedings of the 30th annual conference of the Mathematics Education Research Group of Australasia (MERGA). pp. 805 – 814. Available from http://www.merga.net.au/documents/RP762007.pdf. Last accessed 9/9/10.

Whitin, D.J. and Whitin, P. (2003) Task counts: discussing graphs with young children, *Teaching Mathematics*, 10(13): 142–9.

Wilensky, U. (1991). Abstract meditation on the concrete and concrete implications for mathematics education, in I. Harel and S. Papert (eds) *Constructionism*. Norwood, NJ: Ablex.

Williams, E.M. and Shuard, H. (1970) *Primary Mathematics Today*. London: Longman.

Wood, D. (1998) *How Children Think and Learn*. Oxford: Blackwell Publishers.

Wood, D., Bruner, J.S. and Ross, G. (1979) The role of tutoring in problem solving, *Journal of Child Psychology and Psychiatry*. 17: 89–100.

Yackel, E. and Cobb, P. (1996) Sociomathematical norms, argumentation, and autonomy in mathematics, *Journal for Research in Mathematics Education*, 27(4): 458–77.

Yackel, E., Cobb, P. and Wood, T. (1991) Small-group interactions as a source of learning opportunities in second-grade mathematics, *Journal for Research in Mathematics Education*, 22: 390–408.

Yeo (2008) Teaching Area and Perimeter: Mathematics-Pedagogical-Content Knowledge-in-Action. In M. Goos, R. Brown and K. Makar (Eds.), *Proceedings of the 31st Annual Conference of the Mathematics Education Research Group of Australasia*.

Yin, H.S. (2003) Young children's concept of shape: van Hiele Visualization Level of geometric Thinking. *The Mathematics Educator*, 7(2),71-85 Available from http://repository.nie.edu.sg/jspui/bitstream/10497/65/1/ME-7-2-71.pdf. Last accessed 10/9/10.

Index

Added to a page number 'f' denotes a figure and 't' denotes a table.